CONDENSED WISDOM

A Collection of Aphorisms & Quotations

Composed by Kale Michael Prewitt

Volume I

CONDENSED WISDOM: A COLLECTION OF APHORISMS & QUOTATIONS

For Mom & Dad
I'm forever thankful for your love.

ISBN 978-0-615-63787-7
Printed in the United States of America
October 2012
Second Edition

One could say of me that in this book I have only made up a bunch of other men's flowers, providing of my own only the string to tie them together.

~ Michel de Montaigne ~

TABLE OF CONTENTS

INTRODUCTION

My interest in aphorisms was first sparked by a chance encounter with John Cook's *Positive Quotations* during a time of personal despair, which then lead to an exploration of Christopher Maurer's translation of Baltasar Gracián's *The Art of Worldly Wisdom*. From that point on, I have been hooked on the format of condensed wisdom.

What has attracted me to the art of condensed wisdom is the efficiency and straight-forwardness of its form. While some of even the most brilliant works can provide intermittent nuggets, the aphorism cuts straight to the crux of any conundrum. The aphorism can serve as a gift that continually blossoms in time.

My hope is that the words contained in these works will spur us both onward to further thought, study and growth. I feel truly blessed to have spent the last seven years in study on the works of these great writers. This project has been a labor of love. This book has been solely inspired by intrinsic motivation, but I trust that it will provide some inspiration to others as well.

In this book you will not find the typical positive quotes which pine for some idealistic, perhaps delusional motivation. Instead, many of the selections are gritty, dark and deep. In many ways, these are the unspoken thoughts we deal with in the deep recesses of our minds. I hope these words can serve as a source of hope for even the most cynical among us.

God Bless You in Your Journey,

Kale Michael Prewitt
October 2012

ACTION

Knowledge is not enough, we have to apply it; wanting is not enough, there has to be action.

~Johann Wolfgang von Goethe

Great thoughts speak only to the thoughtful mind, but great actions speak to all mankind.

~Theodore Roosevelt

Action is the antidote to despair.

~Joan Baez

It is better to light a candle than to curse the darkness.

~Chinese proverb

Do the essential things first, and later, if there is time, those that are accessory.

~Baltasar Gracián

The wise do sooner what fools do later.

~Baltasar Gracián

The wise size up immediately what has to be done, sooner or later.

~Baltasar Gracián

Content yourself with doing: leave saying to others.

~Baltasar Gracián

The lazy are always wanting to do something.

~Marquis Vauvenargues

Better to work and fail than to sleep one's life away.

~Jerome K. Jerome

The journey of a thousand miles starts with a single step.

~Chinese Proverb

~

The beginnings of all things are small.

~Cicero

An unfulfilled vocation drains the colour from a man's entire existence.

~Honoré de Balzac

Those that have done nothing in life, are not qualified to judge of those that have done little.

~Samuel Johnson

Nothing will ever be attempted, if all possible objections must be first overcome.

~Samuel Johnson

No one is more liable to make mistakes than the man who acts only on reflection.

~Marquis Vauvenargues

In accomplishing anything definite a man renounces everything else.

~George Santayana

No task is a long one but the task on which one dare not start. It becomes a nightmare.

~Charles Baudelaire

Never undertake anything unless you have the heart to ask Heaven's blessing on your undertaking!

~Georg Christoph Lichtenberg

There is no kind of idleness by which we are so easily seduced as that which dignifies itself by the appearance of business.

~Samuel Johnson

At the day of judgment we shall not be asked what we have read but what we have done.

~Thomas Á Kempis

The best way to avoid a bad action is by doing a good one for there is no difficulty in the world like that of trying to do nothing.

~John Clare

Start by doing what's necessary, then what's possible and suddenly you are doing the impossible.

~Saint Francis of Assisi

Showing up is 80 percent of life.

~Woody Allen

We have got but one life here. It pays, no matter what comes after it, to try and do things, to accomplish things in this life

and not merely to have a soft and pleasant time.

~Theodore Roosevelt

Use well the moment; what the hour

Brings for thy use is in thy power;

And what thou best canst understand

Is just the thing lies nearest to thy hand.

~Johann Wolfgang von Goethe

Life wastes itself whilst we are preparing to live.

~Ralph Waldo Emerson

I AM only one,

But still I am one.

I cannot do everything,

But still I can do something;

And because I cannot do everything

I will not refuse to do the
something that I can do.

~Edward Everett Hale

I must lose myself in action lest
I wither in despair.

~Alfred Lord Tennyson

He who considers too much will
perform little.

~Friedrich Schiller

Action is the proper fruit of
knowledge.

~Thomas Fuller

A man of words and not of
deeds is like a garden full of
weeds.

~Anonymous

Ideas must work through the
brains and arms of men, or they
are no better than dreams.

~Ralph Waldo Emerson

Having ideas is like having
chessmen moving forward; they
may be beaten, but they may
start a winning game.

~Johann Wolfgang von
Goethe

Ennui has made more gamblers
than avarice, more drunkards
than thirst, and perhaps as
many suicides as despair.

~Charles Caleb Colton

ADVERSITY

The best way out is always through.

~Robert Frost

Thy fate is the common fate of all,

Into each life some rain must fall,

Some days must be dark and dreary.

~Henry Wadsworth
Longfellow

Sadness flies away on the wings of time.

~Jean de La Fontaine

How poor are they that have not patience? What wound did ever heal but by degrees?

~William Shakespeare

Necessity makes even the timid brave.

~Sallust

Adversity introduces a man to himself.

~Anonymous

In the depth of winter, I finally learned that there was in me an invincible summer.

~Albert Camus

Forget the times of your distress, but never forget what they taught you.

~Herbert Gasser

A smooth sea never made a skillful mariner.

~English proverb

What does not destroy me makes me stronger.

~Friedrich Nietzsche

A man should learn to sail in all winds.

~Italian Proverb

~

Talents are best nurtured in solitude; character is best formed in the stormy billows of the world.

~Johann Wolfgang von Goethe

The greatest difficulties lie where we are not looking for them.

~Johann Wolfgang von Goethe

Quiet minds cannot be perplexed or frightened but go on in fortune or misfortune at their own private pace, like a clock during a thunderstorm.

~Robert Louis Stevenson

Adversity reminds men of religion.

~Livy

No pain, no palm; no thorns, no throne; no gall, no glory; no cross, no crown.

~William Penn

Idealism increases in direct proportion to one's distance from the problem.

~John Galsworthy

ANGER

Violent men reel from one extremity to another.

~Thomas Fuller II

Anger is never without an argument, but seldom with a good one.

~Marquis of Halifax

A hurtful act is the transference to others of the degradation which we bear in ourselves.

~Simone Weil

People hate those who make them feel their own inferiority.

~Earl of Chesterfield

We boil at different degrees.

~Ralph Waldo Emerson

Anger blows out the lamp of the mind.

~Robert Ingersoll

How much more grievous are the consequences of anger than the causes of it.

~Marcus Aurelius

Anger always thinks it has power beyond its power.

~Publilius Syrus

Who seeks a quarrel, finds it near at hand.

~Italian Proverb

Anger is as a stone cast into a wasp's nest.

~Indian Proverb

To be angry is to revenge the faults of others upon ourselves.

~Alexander Pope

Anger and jealousy can no more bear to lose sight of their objects than love.

~George Eliot

APATHY

Our most powerful emotion is indifference.

> ~Daniel Liebert

There is nothing harder than the softness of indifference.

> ~Juan Montalvo

The opposite of love is not hate, it's indifference.

The opposite of art is not ugliness, it's indifference.

The opposite of faith is not heresy, it's indifference.

And the opposite of life is not death, it's indifference.

> ~Elie Wiesel

~

Beyond a certain pitch of suffering, men are overcome by a kind of ghostly indifference.

> ~Victor Hugo

We care what happens to people only in proportion as we know what people are.

> ~Henry James

The wretched have no compassion.

> ~Samuel Johnson

A corporation cannot blush.

> ~Howel Walsh

If modern civilized man had to keep the animals he eats, the number of vegetarians would rise astronomically.

> ~Christian Morgenstern

APHORISMS

The maxims of men reveal their hearts.

> ~Marquis de
> Vauvenargues

~

The reason for so much outcry against maxims that lay bare the human heart is that people are afraid of having their own laid bare.

> ~ François Duc de la
> Rochefoucauld

Whoever writes in blood and aphorisms does not want to be read but to be learned by heart. In the mountains the shortest way is from peak to peak: but for that one must have long legs. Aphorisms should be peaks - and those who are addressed tall and lofty.

> ~ Friedrich Nietzsche

Good things, when short, are twice as good.

> ~Baltasar Gracián

The great writers of aphorisms read as if they had all known each other well.

> ~Elias Canetti

APPEARANCES

We ought to be such as we
intend to appear.

> ~Benjamin Whichcote

During a carnival men put
cardboard faces over their
masks.

> ~Xavier Forneret

Things pass for what they
seem, not for what they are.
Only rarely do people look
into them, and many are
satisfied with appearances.

> ~Baltasar Gracián

Things do not pass for what
they are, but for what they
seem.

> ~Baltasar Gracián

Things are seldom what they
seem.

> ~Baltasar Gracián

How many people become
abstract as a way of appearing
profound!

> ~Joseph Joubert

~

He who has seen everything
empty itself is close to knowing
what everything is filled with.

> ~Antonio Porchia

A hidden connection is stronger
than an obvious one.

> ~Heraclitus

Our greatest pretenses are built
up not to hide the evil and the
ugly in us, but our emptiness.
The hardest thing to hide is
something that is not there.

> ~Eric Hoffer

11

APPRECIATION

How sharper than a serpent's tooth it is

To have a thankless child.

> ~William Shakespeare

Every man supposes himself not to be fully understood or appreciated.

> ~Ralph Waldo Emerson

~

It is not a failure of others to appreciate your abilities that should trouble you, but rather your failure to appreciate theirs.

> ~Confucius

The deepest principle in human nature is the craving to be appreciated.

> ~William James

If fame is to come only after death, I am in no hurry for it.

> ~Martial

In order to be irreplaceable, one must always be different.

> ~Coco Chanel

Do not cut down the tree that gives you shade.

> ~Arabian Proverb

In everyone there is something precious, found in no one else; so honor each man for what is hidden within him – for what he alone has, and none of his fellows.

> ~Hasidic Proverb

ARGUMENTS

Nothing was ever learned by
either side in a dispute.

~William Hazlitt

The biggest disagreements
appear where the differences
are least.

~Theo Mestrum

~

You have not converted a man
because you have silenced him.

~John Morley

Arguments are to be avoided:
they are always vulgar and
often convincing.

~Oscar Wilde

There is no such test of a man's
superiority of character as in the
well-conducting of an
unavoidable quarrel.

~Sir Henry Taylor

In quarreling, the truth is
always lost.

~Publilius Syrus

The pain of a dispute greatly
outweighs its uses.

~Joseph Joubert

Before you contradict an old
man, my fair friend, you should
endeavor to understand him.

~George Santayana

If you go in for argument, take
care of your temper. Your logic,
if you have any, will take care of
itself.

~Joseph Farrell

Silence is one of the hardest
things to refute.

~Josh Billings

There is no more sense in
having an argument with a man
so stupid he doesn't know you
have the better of him.

~John Roper

We cannot learn from one
another until we stop shouting
at one another – until we speak
quietly enough so that our
words can be heard as well as
our voices.

~Richard Nixon

ART

Where words fail, music speaks.

>~Hans Christian Anderson

>~

Life is short, and art long.

>~Hippocrates

A poet looks at the world as a man looks at a woman.

>~Wallace Stevens

In everything, no matter what it may be, uniformity is undesirable. Leaving something incomplete makes it interesting, and gives one the feeling that there is room for growth.

>~Yoshida Kenkō

Immature poets imitate; mature poets steal.

>~T.S. Eliot

Art is nature speeded up, and God slowed down.

>~Malcolm De Chazal

A film is the world in an hour and a half.

>~Jean~Luc Godard

Cinema should make you forget you're sitting in a theatre.

>~Roman Polanski

A film is a petrified garden of thought.

>~Jean Cocteau

Tragedy is death at the box office.

~Louis B. Mayer

BEAUTY

Beauty is a brief gasp between one cliché and another.

~Ezra Pound

When a rainbow has lasted as long as a quarter hour we stop looking at it.

~Johann Wolfgang von Goethe

Everything has its beauty but not everyone sees it.

~Confucius

The beautiful is as useful as the useful.

~Victor Hugo

~

The most entertaining surface on earth is the human face.

~ Georg Christoph Lichtenberg

Perhaps men who cannot love passionately are those who feel the effect of beauty most keenly; at any rate this is the strongest impression women can make on them.

~Marie-Henri Beyle Stendhal

Men do mightily wrong themselves when they refuse to be present in all ages and neglect to see the beauty of all kingdoms.

~Thomas Traherne

Look twice, if you want a just conception; look once, if what you want is a sense of beauty.

~Henri Frédéric Amiel

There is no excellent beauty that hath not some strangeness in the proportion.

~Francis Bacon

The beautiful souls are they that are universal, open, and ready for all things.

~Michel de Montaigne

The best part of beauty is that which no picture can express.

~Francis Bacon

Youth is happy because it has the ability to see beauty. Anyone who keeps the ability to see beauty never grows old.

~Franz Kafka

BELIEFS

Nothing is more dangerous than an idea when it's the only one we have.

> ~ Émile Chartier Alain

You really only know when you know little; doubt grows with knowledge.

> ~Johann Wolfgang von Goethe

Doubt is not a pleasant state, but certainty is a ridiculous one.

> ~Voltaire

~

Convictions are more dangerous enemies of truth than lies.

> ~Friedrich Nietzsche

Only so far as a man believes strongly, mightily, can he act cheerfully, or do anything worth doing.

> ~Frederick W. Robertson

The man who cannot believe in himself cannot believe in anything else.

> ~Roy L. Smith

Nothing is so firmly believed as what is least known.

> ~Michel de Montaigne

It is almost impossible to state what one in fact believes because it is almost impossible to hold a belief and to define it at the same time.

> ~William Carlos Williams

A definition is the enclosing of a wilderness of ideas within a wall of words.

~Samuel Butler

A fanatic is one who sticks to his guns, whether they're loaded or not.

~Franklin Jones

He does not believe that does not live according to his belief.

~Thomas Fuller

The Skeptics that affirmed they knew nothing, even in that opinion confused themselves and thought they knew more than all the world beside.

~Sir Thomas Browne

BOOKS

Wherever they burn books
they will also, in the end, burn
human beings.

~Heinrich Heine

One of the conditions for
reading what is good is that we
must not read what is bad; for
life is short and time and
energy are limited.

~Arthur Schopenhauer

No furniture so charming as
books.

~Sydney Smith

The author must keep his
mouth shut when his work
starts to speak.

~ Friedrich Nietzsche

~

A classic is something that
everyone wants to have read
and nobody wants to read.

~Mark Twain

Let us see the result of good
food in a strong body, and the
result of great reading in a full
and powerful mind.

~Sydney Smith

Reading means borrowing.

~Georg Christoph
Lichtenberg

A book is like a garden carried
in the pocket.

~Anonymous

A room without books is a body
without a soul.

~Cicero

No book is really worth reading at the age of ten which is not equally, and often far more, worth reading at the age of fifty and beyond.

~C.S. Lewis

The learned fool writes his nonsense in better language than the unlearned, but it is still nonsense.

~Ben Franklin

If we encounter a man of rare intellect we should ask him what books he reads.

~Ralph Waldo Emerson

Read, mark, learn, and inwardly digest.

~The Book of Common Prayer

CHANGE

Begin to be now what you will be hereafter.

~William James

Begin doing what you want to do *now*.

~Marie Beynon Ray

There is in the worst of fortune the best of chances for a happy change.

~Euripides

The second step in the right direction is the most difficult.

~Theo Mestrum

Change is not progress.

~H.L. Mencken

Repetition is the only form of permanence that nature can achieve.

~George Santayana

Nothing endures but change.

~Heraclitus

God grant me the serenity to accept the things I cannot change, courage to change the things I can, and wisdom to know the difference.

~Reinhold Niebuhr

Just improve yourself; that is the only thing you can do to better the world.

~Ludwig Wittgenstein

~

We can't form our children on our own concepts; we must take

them and love them as God
gives them to us.

> ~Johann Wolfgang von
> Goethe

Everyone has it within his
power to say, this I am today,
that I shall be tomorrow.

> ~Louis L'Amour

If you want to make enemies,
try to change something.

> ~Woodrow Wilson

We must always change, renew,
rejuvenate ourselves; otherwise
we harden.

> ~Johann Wolfgang von
> Goethe

COMPASSION

The highest ecstasy is the attention at its fullest.

> ~Simone Weil

You can rarely trouble another without feeling troubled, either by pity or by remorse.

> ~Baltasar Gracián

There is no one who cannot better someone else at something.

> ~Baltasar Gracián

Nothing is more characteristic of a man than the manner in which he behaves toward fools.

> ~Henri-Frédéric Amie

~

Magnanimity has no need to prove the prudence of its motives.

> ~Marquis Vauvenargues

Don't use the impudence of a beggar as an excuse for not helping him.

> ~Rabbi Shmelke of Nicolsburg

Compassion is the chief law of human existence.

> ~Fyodor Dostoevsky

More helpful than all wisdom or counsel is one draught of simple human pity that will not forsake us.

> ~George Eliot

When I see the ten most wanted list, I always have this thought,

if we'd made them feel wanted
earlier, they wouldn't be
wanted now.

~Eddie Cantor

He jests at scars that never felt a
wound.

~William Shakespeare

CONTENTMENT

Contentment is natural wealth;
luxury is artificial poverty.

~Socrates

We know nothing of
tomorrow; our business is to be
good and happy today.

~Sydney Smith

No lure is greater than to
possess what others want, no
disaster greater than not to be
content with what one has.

~Lao Tzu

Nothing is sufficient for the
man to whom the sufficient is
too little.

~ Epicurus

Here with a loaf of bread
beneath the bough,
A flask of wine, a book of
verse - and thou

Beside me singing in the
wilderness -
And wilderness is enow.

~ Edward FitzGerald

The land of discontent is a
spacious one, filled with
monsters.

~Baltasar Gracián

Nothing is enough for the man
for whom enough is too little.

~Epicurus

No longer forward nor behind
I look in hope or fear;

But grateful, take the good I
find, the best of now and here.

~John Greenleaf
Whittier

The grand essentials in this life
are something to do, something

to love, and something to hope for.

~Joseph Addison

~

Winter is in my head, but spring is in my heart.

~Victor Hugo

Cheerfulness means a contented spirit, a pure heart, a kind and loving disposition; it means humility and charity, a generous appreciation of others, and a modest opinion of self.

~William Makepeace Thackeray

Of the blessings set before you, make your choice and be content.

~Samuel Johnson

However mean your life is, meet it and live it; do not shun it and call it names. It looks poorest when you are richest. The fault-finder will find faults even in paradise. Love your life.

~Henry David Thoreau

Blessed be he who expects nothing, for he shall never be disappointed.

~Alexander Pope

~Jonathan Swift

He who prizes little things is worthy of great ones.

~German Proverb

When we cannot find contentment in ourselves, it is useless to seek it elsewhere.

~ François Duc de la Rochefoucauld

A long life may not be good enough, but a good life is long enough.

~Anonymous

~D. Jerrard

Happiness grows at our own
firesides and is not to be picked
in strangers' gardens.

CONVERSATION

When people talk to me about
the weather, I always feel they
mean something else.

~Oscar Wilde

~

To do all the talking and not be
willing to listen is a form of
greed.

~Democritus of Abdera

There are people who instead of
listening to what is being said to
them are already listening to
what they are going to say
themselves.

~Albert Guinon

If we would please in society,
we must be prepared to be
taught many things we know
already by people who do not
know them.

~Sébastien Nicolas
Roche Chamfort

He has occasional flashes of
silence that make his
conversation perfectly
delightful.

~Sydney Smith

Wise men talk because they
have something to say; fools,
because they have to say
something.

~Plato

The empty vessel makes the
greatest sound.

~William Shakespeare

The wise man has long ears, big
eyes and a short tongue.

~Russian Proverb

30

We have two ears and one
mouth that we may listen the
more and talk the less.

~Greek Proverb

Give every man thine ear, but
few thy voice.

~William Shakespeare

Eavesdroppers never hear any
good of themselves.

~French Proverb

And he goes through life, his
mouth open, and his mind
closed.

~Oscar Wilde

Hearts that are delicate and
kind and tongues that are
neither – these make the finest
company in the world.

~Logan Pearsall Smith

The most precious things in
speech are pauses.

~Ralph Richardson

Silence is one great art of
conversation.

~William Hazlitt

Silence may be as variously
shaded as speech.

~Edith Wharton

COWARDICE

It is hard to fail, but it is worse
never to have tried to succeed.

> ~Theodore Roosevelt

Cowards die many times
before their deaths; the valiant
never taste of death but once.

> ~William Shakespeare

Any coward can fight a battle
when he's sure of winning.

> ~George Eliot

To persevere, trusting in what
hopes he has, is courage. The
coward despairs.

> ~Euripides

It's weak and despicable to go
on wanting things and not
trying to get them.

> ~Joanna Field

I love the man that can smile in
trouble, that can gather
strength from distress, and
grow brave by reflection.

> ~Thomas Paine

Many would be cowards if
they had courage enough.

> ~Thomas Fuller

Patience and fortitude conquer
all things.

> ~Ralph Waldo Emerson

I beg you take courage; the
brave soul can mend even
disaster.

> ~Catherine of Russia

If the sky falls, hold up your
hands.

> ~Spanish Proverb

Courage is resistance to fear, mastery of fear, not absence of fear.

> ~Mark Twain

The best help is not to bear the troubles of others for them, but to **inspire them with courage and energy to bear their burdens** for themselves and meet the difficulties of life bravely.

> ~Sir John Lubbock

~

It is with trifles, and when he is off guard, that a man best reveals his character.

> ~Arthur Schopenhauer

Fortunately for themselves and the world, nearly all men are cowards and dare not act on what they believe. Nearly all our disasters come of a few fools having the "courage of their convictions."

> ~Coventry Patmore

The powers of the soul are commensurate with its needs.

> ~Ralph Waldo Emerson

Keep your fears to yourself, but share your courage with others.

> ~Robert Louis Stevenson

Occasions do not make a man either strong or weak, but they show what he is.

> ~Thomas à Kempis

Facing it, always facing it, that's the way to get through. Face it.

> ~Joseph Conrad

Each time a man stands up for an ideal, or acts to improve the lot of others, or strikes out against injustice, he sends forth a tiny ripple of hope … and crossing each other from a million different centers of

33

energy and daring, those ripples
build a current that can sweep
down the mightiest walls of
oppression and resistance.

~Robert F. Kennedy

I would define courage to be a
perfect sensibility of the
measure of danger, and a
mental willingness to endure it.

~General William
Sherman

Curiosity will conquer fear even
more than bravery will.

~James Stephens

CREATION

The best ideas are common property.

~Seneca

What actually is invention? It is the conclusion of what has been sought.

~Johann Wolfgang von Goethe

Before it is, everything is not, and when it begins to be, it is still very close to non-being.

~Baltasar Gracián

Few are those who see with their own eyes and feel with their own hearts.

~Albert Einstein

Originality is undetected plagiarism.

~Ralph William Inge

~

A creator needs only one enthusiast to justify him.

~Man Ray

Power is much more easily manifested in destroying than in creating.

~William Wordsworth

Originality does not consist in saying what no one has ever said before, but in saying exactly what you think yourself.

~J.F. Stephen

The least of things with a meaning is worth more in life than the greatest of things without it.

~Carl Gustav Jung

CRUELTY

Silence is the most perfect
expression of scorn.

> ~George Bernard Shaw

The cruelest lies are often told
in silence.

> ~Robert Louis
> Stevenson

You can't hold a man down
without staying down with
him.

> ~Booker T. Washington

Cruelty isn't softened by tears;
it feeds on them.

> ~Publilius Syrus

There is no reply so sharp as
silent contempt.

> ~Michel de Montaigne

~

When a mean person plans to
injure a gentleman, his heart is
cruel, his plans are well laid out
and his action is firm; therefore
the gentleman can seldom
escape. When a gentleman
intends to punish a mean
person, his heart is kind, his
plans are incomplete, and he
cannot quite go the limit;
therefore more often he himself
is victimized by it.

> ~'Mr. Tut-Tut'

DEATH

Man does not fear death, only the suffering.

~Witold Gombrowicz

It is of no avail to weep for the loss of a loved one, which is why we weep.

~Solon

In every parting there is an image of death.

~George Eliot

Until death, it is all life.

~Miguel de Cervantes

While I thought that I was learning how to live, I have been learning how to die.

~Leonardo da Vinci

No man should be afraid to die, who hath understood what it is to live.

~Thomas Fuller

Every day is a little life;

Every waking and rising a little birth,

Every fresh morning a little youth,

Every going to rest and sleep a little death.

~Arthur Schopenhauer

If a man hasn't discovered something that he will die for, he isn't fit to live.

~Martin Luther King, Jr.

~

The hour which gives us life begins to take it away.

~Seneca

Why do dying people never
shed tears?

~Max Frisch

All I desire for my own burial is
not to be buried alive.

~Lord Chesterfield

We sometimes congratulate
ourselves at the moment of
waking from a troubled dream;
it may be so the moment after
death.

~Nathaniel Hawthorne

One must not become attached
to animals: they do not last long
enough. Or to men: they last
too long.

~Anonymous

It matters not how a man dies,
but how he lives.

~Samuel Johnson

Into the darkness they go, the
wise and the lovely.

~Edna St. Vincent
Millay

It is not death that alarms me,
but dying.

~Michel de Montaigne

The good man should go on
living as long as he ought to, not
just as long as he likes.

~Seneca

If some persons died, and others
did not die, death would indeed
be a terrible affliction.

~Jean de La Bruyère

The fall of a leaf is a whisper to
the living.

~Russian Proverb

To live in hearts we leave
behind is not to die.

~Anonymous

Our lives are but our marches to our graves.

~John Fletcher

Life is real! Life is earnest!

And the grave is not its goal;

Dust thou art, to dust returnest,

Was not spoken of the soul.

Tell me not, in mournful numbers,

Life is but an empty dream!

For the soul is dead that slumbers,

And things are not what they seem.

~Henry Wadsworth
Longfellow

DECEPTION

He who promises everything promises nothing; promises are a trap for fools.

~Baltasar Gracián

~

A flatterer is a man that tells you your opinion and not his own.

~Anonymous

He who knows how to flatter also knows how to slander.

~Napoleon Bonaparte

Hypocrisy is the most difficult and nerve-racking vice that any man can pursue; it needs an unceasing vigilance and a rare detachment of spirit. It cannot, like adultery or gluttony, be practiced at spare moments; it is a whole-time job.

~Somerset Maugham

It is not in human nature to deceive others, for any long time, without in a measure, deceiving ourselves.

~J.H. Newman

We ought to see far enough into a hypocrite to see even his sincerity.

~G.K. Chesterton

The world wants to be deceived.

~Sebastian Brant

He who is not very strong in memory should not meddle with lying.

~ Michel de Montaigne

Who lies for you will lie against you.

~Bosnian proverb

Learn how to refuse favors. This is a great and very useful art.

~Thomas Fuller

Always mistrust a subordinate who never finds fault with his superior.

~John Churton Collins

You may be deceived if you trust too much, but you will live in torment if you do not trust enough.

~Frank Crane

We are never deceived. We deceive ourselves.

~Johann Wolfgang von Goethe

It is a double pleasure to deceive the deceiver.

~Jean de La Fontaine

When a man is really important, the worst adviser he can have is a flatterer.

~Anonymous

It is more shameful to distrust one's friends than to be deceived by them.

~François Duc de la Rochefoucauld

He who tells a lie is not sensible of how great a task he undertakes; for he must be forced to invent twenty more to maintain that one.

~Alexander Pope

Half the truth is often a great lie.

~Benjamin Franklin

The great masses of the people will more easily fall victims to a big lie than to a small one.

~Adolf Hitler

~Georg Christoph Lichtenberg

It is better to suffer wrong than to do it, and happier to be sometimes cheated than not to trust.

~Samuel Johnson

Trust, like the soul, never returns, once it is gone.

~Publilius Syrus

The fly that does not want to be swatted is safest if it sits on the fly-swat.

Innocence itself sometimes hath need of a mask.

~English proverb

Make thyself a sheep, and the wolf is ready.

~Russian Proverb

DECISIONS

Decide which is the line of conduct that presents the fewest drawbacks and then follow it out as being the best one, because one never finds anything perfectly pure and unmixed, or exempt from danger.

~Niccolò Machiavelli

Necessity saves us the trouble of choosing.

~Marquis de Vauvenargues

~

Necessity relieves us from the embarrassment of choice.

~Marquis de Vauvenargues

Wherever a man may happen to turn, whatever a man may undertake, he will always end up returning to that path which nature has marked out for him.

~Johann Wolfgang von Goethe

Endurance is frequently a form of indecision.

~Elizabeth Bibesco

Blessed is he who has reached the point of no return and knows it, for he shall enjoy living.

~William Bennett

Grub first, then ethics.

~Bertold Brecht

DESIRES

Our desires always increases with our possessions. The knowledge that something remains yet unenjoyed impairs our enjoyment of the good before us.

~Samuel Johnson

It is in no man's power to have whatever he wants; but he has it in his power not to wish for what he hasn't got, and cheerfully make the most of the things that do come his way.

~ Seneca

Possessions are generally diminished by possession.

~Friedrich Nietzsche

Fear begins where desire ends.

~Baltasar Gracián

Latent in every man is a venom of amazing bitterness, a black resentment; something that curses and loathes life, a feeling of being trapped, of having trusted and been fooled, of being the helpless prey of impotent rage, blind surrender, the victim of a savage, ruthless power that gives and takes away, enlists a man, drops him, promises and betrays, and – crowning injury – inflicts on him the humiliation of feeling sorry for himself and of regarding this 'power' as an intelligent, sentient being, capable of being touched.

~Paul Valéry

~

As long as the heart preserves desire, the mind preserves illusion.

~François-René de Chateaubriand

What nature requires is obtainable, and within easy reach. It's for the superfluous we sweat.

~Seneca

The things we are best acquainted with are often the things we lack. This is because we have spent so much time thinking of them.

~Gerald Brenan

Limited in his nature, infinite in his desires, man is a fallen god who remembers heaven.

~Alphonse de
Lamartine

Man is an intellectual animal, and therefore an everlasting contradiction to himself.

~William Hazlitt

With everything that we do, we desire more or less the end; we are impatient to be done with it and glad when it is finished. It is only the end in general, the end of all ends, that we wish, as a rule, to put off as long as possible.

~Arthur Schopenhauer

I can't tell if a straw ever saved a drowning man, but I know that a mere glance is enough to make despair pause. For in truth we who are creatures of impulse are not creatures of despair.

~Joseph Conrad

On the brink of being satiated, desire still appears infinite.

~Jean Rostand

There is nothing like desire for preventing the things we say from having any resemblance to the things in our minds.

~Marcel Proust

Freedom is not procured by a
full enjoyment of what is
desired, but by controlling that
desire.

~Epictetus

He who desires, but acts not,
breeds pestilence.

~William Blake

Desire is half of life; indifference
is half of death.

~Kahlil Gibran

Desire beautifies what is ugly.

~Spanish Proverb

Life contains but two tragedies.
One is not to get your heart's
desire; the other is to get it.

~Socrates

EDUCATION

Educate the children and it won't be necessary to punish the men.

~Pythagoras

Crafty men condemn studies; simple men admire them, and wise men use them.

~Francis Bacon

If you think education is expensive, try ignorance.

~Derek Bok

~

Human history becomes more and more a race between education and catastrophe.

~H.G. Wells

Education is the ability to listen to almost anything without losing your temper or self-confidence.

~Anonymous

Education is a state controlled manufactory of echoes.

~Norman Douglas

ENEMIES

The noblest kind of retribution is not to become like your enemy.

~Marcus Aurelius

You can discover what your enemy fears most by observing the means he uses to frighten you.

~Eric Hoffer

Treat people as if they were what they ought to be and you help them become what they are capable of becoming.

~Johann Wolfgang von Goethe

The antidote for fifty enemies is one friend.

~Aristotle

~

It is seldom indeed that one parts on good terms, because if one were on good terms one would not part.

~Marcel Proust

A man cannot be too careful in the choice of his enemies.

~Oscar Wilde

If you injure your neighbor, better not do it by halves.

~George Bernard Shaw

There is nothing so common as to imitate the practice of enemies and to use their weapons.

~Voltaire

Search thy own heart; what paineth thee in others, in thyself may be.

~John Greenleaf
Whittier

We has met the enemy, and it is
us.

~Walt Kelly

Beat not the furnace for your foe
so hot that it do singe yourself.

~William Shakespeare

If you have to kill a snake, kill it
once and for all.

~Japanese Proverb

Do not despise an insignificant
enemy or a slight wound.

~German Proverb

It is discouraging to try and be a
good neighbor in a bad
neighborhood.

~William Castle

Get acquainted with your
neighbor; you might like him.

~Father H.B. Tierney

EXPECTATIONS

Prospect is often better than possession.

~Thomas Fuller

Leave nectar on their lips.

~Baltasar Gracián

A cathedral, a wave of a storm, a dancer's leap, never turn out to be as high as we had hoped.

~Marcel Proust

When a man forgets his ideals, he may hope for happiness, but not till then.

~John Oliver Hobbes

~

I am a man; I consider nothing foreign to me.

~ Terence

The greatest evil that fortune can bring men is to endow them with feeble resources and yet to make them ambitious.

~ Marquis de Vauvenargues

All expectation hath something of torment.

~Benjamin Whichcote

Perfection of means and confusion of ends seem to characterize our age.

~Albert Einstein

One ought not to desire the impossible.

~Leonardo da Vinci

Life is made up of interruptions.

~W.S. Gilbert

FAILURE

Only he who does nothing
makes no mistakes.

> ~French proverb

Defeat in doing right is
nevertheless victory.

> ~Frederick W.
> Robertson

Those who try and fail are
much wiser than those who
never try for fear of failure.

> ~Andre Bustanoby

We fail more often by timidity
than by over-daring.

> ~David Grayson

I would prefer even to fail with
honor than win by cheating.

> ~Sophocles

How many pessimists end up
desiring the things they fear, in
order to prove that they are
right.

> ~Robert Mallet

Our greatest glory is not in
never falling, but in rising
every time we fall.

> ~Confucius

Much does he gain who learns
when he loses.

> ~Miguel de Cervantes

Failure isn't terrible if you can
say to yourself, hey, **I know I'm
gonna be successful at what I
want to do someday**. Failure
doesn't become a big hangup
then because it's only
temporary. If failure is
absolute, then it would be
disaster, but as long as it's only

51

temporary you can just go and achieve almost anything.

~Jerry Della Femina

~

We are dismayed when we find that even disaster cannot cure us of our faults.

~Marquis Vauvenargues

Experience is the name everyone gives to his mistakes.

~Oscar Wilde

It is often the failure who is the pioneer in new lands, new undertakings, and new forms of expression.

~Eric Hoffer

The common idea that success spoils people by making them vain, egotistic, and self-complacent is erroneous; on the contrary, it makes them, for the most part, humble, tolerant, and kind. Failure makes people cruel and bitter.

~Somerset Maugham

Have gratitude for what you have and forgive yourself for what might have been. We are all failures in one way or another, but failure is more than the end of something. It is the opportunity to begin something else. Enjoy your successes, accept your failures. Move on from both. But keep moving on.

~Michael Ian Black

Experience is a jewel, and it had need to be so, for it is often purchased at an infinite rate.

~William Shakespeare

Experience is not what happens to you. It is what you do with what happens to you.

~Aldous Huxley

Experience is the name men give to their follies or their sorrows.

~Alfred De Musset

Failure has no friends.

~John F. Kennedy

Notice the difference between what happens when a man says to himself, 'I have failed three times' and what happens when he says 'I am a failure.'

~S.I. Hayakawa

There is no formula for success. But there is a formula for failure and that is trying to please everybody.

~Man Ray

FAME

Wealth is like sea-water; the more we drink, the thirstier we become; and the same is true of fame.

~Arthur Schopenhauer

Avoid shame, but do not seek glory; nothing so expensive as glory.

~Sydney Smith

Most celebrated men live in a condition of prostitution.

~Sainte-Beuve

Fools invent fashions, and wise men are fain to follow them.

~Samuel Butler (I)

Fashion, *n.* A despot whom the wise ridicule and obey.

~Ambrose Bierce

Dress is a very foolish thing, and yet it is a very foolish thing for a man not to be well dressed.

~Lord Chesterfield

Why long for glory, which one despises as soon as one has it? But that is precisely what the ambitious man wants; having it in order to be able to despise it.

~Jean Rostand

Popularity is a crime from the moment it is sought; it is only a virtue where men have it whether they will or no.

~Lord Halifax

If you would not be forgotten as soon as you are dead, either write things worth reading or do things worth writing.

~Benjamin Franklin

How many people live on the
reputation of the reputation
they might have made.

~Oliver Wendell
Holmes

A fashion is nothing but an
induced epidemic.

~George Bernard Shaw

Fashion is a form of ugliness so
intolerable that we have to alter
it every six months.

~Oscar Wilde

FEAR

In misfortune we usually regain the peace that we were robbed of through the fear of that very misfortune.

~Marie von Ebner-Eschenbach

When there is less fear, there is less danger.

~Francisco de Quevedo

He who has overcome his fears will truly be free.

~Aristotle

To relinquish a present good through apprehension of a future evil is in most instances unwise ... from a fear which may afterwards turn out groundless, you lost the good that lay within your grasp.

~Francesco Guicciardini

He who fears he shall suffer, already suffers what he fears.

~Michel de Montaigne

There is nothing that fear or hope does not make men believe.

~Vauvenargues

Fear, if allowed free rein, would reduce all of us to trembling shadows of men, for whom only death could bring release.

~John M. Wilson

Fear makes the wolf bigger than he is.

~German proverb

He who foresees calamities suffers them twice over.

~Beilby Porteus

He who fears he shall suffer
already suffers what he fears.

~Michel de Montaigne

Many perished from what they
feared, but what good was
fearing it when they took no
steps to prevent it?

~Baltasar Gracián

What was feared as ruinous
comes to seem tolerable.

~Baltasar Gracián

The first duty for a man is still
that of subduing *Fear*.

~Thomas Carlyle

To the man who is afraid,
everything rustles.

~Sophocles

To conquer fear is the
beginning of wisdom.

~Bertrand Russell

~

The fear of separation is all that
unites.

~Antonio Porchia

Men are more ready to offend
one who desires to be beloved
than one who wishes to be
feared.

~Niccolò Machiavelli

All things are less dreadful than
they seem.

~Anonymous

We fear something before we
hate it. A child who fears noises
becomes a man that hates
noises.

~Cyril Connolly

We have to realize that we are
as deeply afraid to live and to
love as we are to die.

~R.D. Laing   ~Eric Hoffer

Fear of becoming a has-been   Let them hate, so long as they
keeps some people from   fear.
becoming anything.
                                                              ~Lucius Accius

FOLLY

Three classes of fools:

Men because of pride,

Girls by love,

Women by jealousy.

> ~Johann Wolfgang von
> Goethe

The following are mad:

He who tries to teach
simpletons,

Contradicts the wise,

Is moved by empty speeches

Believes whores

Entrusts secrets to the
garrulous

> ~Johann Wolfgang von
> Goethe

But who will correct all this
common folly?

> ~Baltasar Gracián

Never stumble over fools.

> ~Baltasar Gracián

Any foolishness is vulgarity,
and the vulgar are composed of
fools.

> ~Baltasar Gracián

Don't turn one act of
foolishness into two.

> ~Baltasar Gracián

Don't persist in folly. Some
people commit themselves to
their errors. They act
mistakenly and consider it
constancy to go on that way.

> ~Baltasar Gracián

Scoundrels are always sociable.

> ~Arthur Schopenhauer

~

59

~G.K. Chesterton

Weak men are the worse for the good sense they read in books because it furnisheth them only with more matter to mistake.

~Marquess of Halifax

Weak people never give way when they ought to.

~Jean François Paul de Gondi

It is better to speak wisdom foolishly, like the saints, rather than to speak folly wisely, like the dons.

To make a trade of laughing at a fool is the highway to becoming one.

~Thomas Fuller

The voice of intelligence … is drowned out by the roar of fear … Most of all it is silenced by ignorance.

~Karl Menninger

FORGIVENESS

Nor can we fall below the arms
of God, how low soever it be
we fall.

~William Penn

~

It is much easier to repent of
sins that we have committed
than to repent of those we
intend to commit.

~Josh Billings

Nobody ever forgets where he
buried the hatchet.

~Kin Hubbard

Teach me to feel another's woe,

To hide the fault I see;

That mercy I to others show,

That mercy show to me.

~Alexander Pope

The more a man knows, the
more he forgives.

~Anonymous

Don't see all you see, and don't
hear all you hear.

~Irish Proverb

He who has not forgiven an
enemy has not yet tasted one of
the most sublime enjoyments of
life.

~Johann Kaspar Lavater

Let not men's sin dishearten
thee: love a man even in his sin,
for that love is a likeness of the
divine love, and is the summit
of love on earth.

~Feodor Dostoevsky

FREEDOM

Freedom stretches as far as
your self-control.

> ~Marie von Ebner-
> Eschenbach

We must free ourselves from
the prison of everyday affairs
and politics.

> ~Epicurus

Freedom is only good as a
means; it is no end in itself.

~Herman Melville

~

A man's worst difficulties begin
when he is able to do as he likes.

> ~T.H. Huxley

Nothing really sets human
nature free but self control.

> ~Paul Bottome

FRIENDSHIP

The only safe and sure way to destroy an enemy is to make him your friend.

> ~Mark Twain

Go often to the house of a friend for weeds choke the unused path.

> ~Ralph Waldo Emerson

Tell me with whom you consort and I will tell you who you are; if I know how you spend your time, then I know what might become of you.

> ~Johann Wolfgang von Goethe

The only way to have a friend is to be one.

> ~Ralph Waldo Emerson

~

Three things are not recognized except in the due course of time:

A hero in wartime

A wise man in a rage,

A friend in need

> ~Johann Wolfgang von Goethe

A guest sticks a nail in the wall even if he stays but one night.

> ~Polish proverb

Friendship cannot live with ceremony, nor without civility.

> ~William Halifax

Everybody's friend is nobody's.

> ~ Arthur Schopenhauer

Friendship is like money, easier made than kept.

~Samuel Butler

Each has his past shut in him like the leaves of a book shown to him by heart, and his friends can only read the title.

~Virginia Woolf

True friends visit us in prosperity only when invited, but in adversity they come without invitation.

~Theophrastus

The mind is rarely so disturbed, but that the company of a friend will restore it to some degree of tranquility and sedateness.

~Adam Smith

Don't abuse your friends and expect them to consider it criticism.

~E.W. Howe

Don't go to visit a friend in the hour of his disgrace.

~Rabbi Ben Eleazer

In prosperity our friends know us; in adversity we know our friends.

~John Churton Collins

Grief can take care of itself, but to get the full value of joy you must have somebody to divide it with.

~Mark Twain

Go forth into the busy world and love it. Interest yourself in life, mingle kindly with its joys and sorrows, try what you can do for others rather than what you can make them do for you, and you will know what it is to have friends.

~Ralph Waldo Emerson

Friend is sometimes a word devoid of meaning; *enemy*, never.

~Victor Hugo

It takes your enemy and your friend, working together, to hurt you to the heart; the one to slander you and the other to get the news to you.

~Mark Twain

He that advised thee not to let sun set on thine anger did not command thee to trust a deceiving enemy the next morning.

~Thomas Fuller

The art of living is more like wrestling than dancing.

~Marcus Aurelius

There is no one who does not represent a danger to someone.

~Madame de Sévigné

All our foes are mortal.

~Paul Valéry

There is no finer revenge than that which *others* inflict on your enemy. Moreover, it has the advantage of leaving you the role of a generous man.

~Cesare Pavese

Man is a social animal who dislikes his fellow men.

~Eugène Delacroix

Better lose a jest than a friend.

~Thomas Fuller

Friend: one who knows all about you and loves you just the same.

~Elbert Hubbard

Without friends, the world is but a wilderness.

~Francis Bacon

It is not so much our friends'
help that helps us as the
confident knowledge that they
will help us.

~Epicurus

~Benjamin Franklin

Life without a friend, death
without a witness.

~George Herbert

There are three faithful friends –
an old wife, an old dog, and
ready money.

GIVING

When you rise in the morning, form a resolution to make the day a happy one for a fellow creature.

~Sydney Smith

Who does not in some sort live to others, does not live much to himself.

~Michel de Montaigne

Do good with what thou hast, or it will do thee no good.

~William Penn

A man there was and they called him mad; the more he gave the more he had.

~John Bunyan

They who give have all things; they who withhold have nothing.

~Hindu Proverb

It is not only what we do, but also what we do not do, for which we are accountable.

~ Molière

The only gift is a portion of thyself.

~Ralph Waldo Emerson

Happiness is a perfume you cannot pour on others without getting a few drops on yourself.

~Ralph Waldo Emerson

I expect to pass through life but once.
If, therefore, there be any kindness I can show, or any good thing I can do to any fellow being, let me do it now, for I shall not pass this way again.

~William Penn

The impersonal hand of government can never replace the helping hand of a neighbor.

~Hubert H. Humphrey

Do not choose for anyone what you do not choose for yourself.

~Persian Proverb

~

No one is useless in this world who lightens the burden of it to any one else.

~Charles Dickens

He who plants trees loves others besides himself.

~Anonymous

He who allows his day to pass by without practicing generosity and enjoying life's pleasures is like a blacksmith's bellows – he breathes but does not live.

~Sanskrit Proverb

He who plants thorns must never expect to gather roses.

~Arabian Proverb

To sow is less difficult than to reap.

~Johann Wolfgang von Goethe

When a father gives to his son, both laugh; when a son gives to his father, both cry.

~Yiddish proverb

If you have built castles in the air,
Your work need not be lost;
That is where they should be.
Now put the foundations under them.

~Henry David Thoreau

GOALS

First say to yourself what you would be, and then do what you have to do.

~Epictetus

Ideals are like stars: You will not succeed in touching them with your hands, but like the seafaring man on the desert of waters, you choose them as your guides, and following them, you reach your destiny.

~Carl Schurz

Make a plan, one that is full of obtainable goals for a happy life. Read through that plan daily so that it becomes a permanent part of your thought process.

~Sara Henderson

Just don't give up trying to do what you really want to do. When there is love and inspiration, I don't think you can go far wrong.

~Ella Fitzgerald

Not every end is a goal. The end of a melody is not its goal; but nonetheless, if a melody had not reached its end it would not have reached its goal either. A parable.

~Friedrich Nietzsche

GOD

The riddles of God are more satisfying than the solutions of man.

~G.K. Chesterton

We have just enough religion to make us hate, but not enough to make us love another.

~Jonathan Swift

Let nothing disturb thee, nothing affright thee;

All things are passing; God never changeth;

Patient endurance attaineth all things;

Who God possesseth in nothing is wanting;

Alone God sufficeth.

~Henry Wadsworth Longfellow

~Santa Teresa

The cask can only yield the wine it contains.

~Italian Proverb

The best way to know God is to love many things.

~Vincent van Gogh

'Nature hides God!' But not from everyone!

~Johann Wolfgang von Goethe

~

God builds his temple in the heart
On the ruins of churches and religions.
~ Ralph Waldo Emerson

We dance around in a ring and suppose,

But the Secret sits in the middle and knows.

~Robert Frost

The knowledge of God is very far from the love of Him.

~Blaise Pascal

It always strikes me, and it is very peculiar, that, whenever we see the image of indescribable and unutterable desolation – of loneliness, poverty, and misery, the end and extreme of things – the thought of God comes into one's mind.

~Vincent Van Gogh

God enters by a private door into every individual.

~Ralph Waldo Emerson

Be not afraid to pray; to pray is right.

Pray if thou canst, with hope, but ever pray,

Though hope be weak, or sick with long delay,

Pray in the darkness if there be no light.

~Hartley Coleridge

God dwells wherever man lets him in.

~Mendel of Kotzk

God wants the heart.

~The Talmud

He who knows about depth, knows about God.

~Paul Tillich

The universe is one of God's thoughts.

~Friedrich von Schiller

The greatest act of faith is when man decides he is not God.

~Oliver Wendell Holmes

GOOD & EVIL

Ignorance is the mother of all
evils.

~Michel de Montaigne

Fear is pain arising from the
anticipation of evil.

~Aristotle

There is nothing that doesn't
have something good.

~Baltasar Gracián

He that can lick can bite.

~French proverb

How far that little candle
throws his beams! So shines a
good deed in a naughty world.

~William Shakespeare

Justice is like a train that's
nearly always late.

~Yevgeny Yevtushenko

~

The wicked are always
surprised to find that the good
can be clever.

~Marquis
Vauvenargues

You cannot have power for
good without having power for
evil too. Even mother's milk
nourishes murderers as well as
heroes.

~George Bernard Shaw

Cruelty isn't softened by tears, it
feeds on them.

~Publilius Syrus

Scarce anything awakens
attention like a tale of cruelty.

~Samuel Johnson

Where the generality are offenders, justice cometh to be cruelty.

~Marquess of Halifax

Fine minds are seldom fine souls.

~Jean Paul Richter

Our actions are neither so good nor so evil as our impulses.

~Marquis de Vauvenargues

The world is the best of all possible worlds, and *everything* in it is a necessary evil.

~Francis Herbert Bradley

Man is almost always as wicked as his needs required.

~Giacomo Leopardi

There are bad people who would be less dangerous if they had no good in them.

~François Duc de la Rochefoucauld

I never wonder to see men wicked, but I often wonder to see them unashamed.

~Jonathan Swift

Bad nature never lacks an instructor.

~Publilius Syrus

Evil comes at leisure like the disease; good comes in a hurry like the doctor.

~G.K. Chesterton

We have neither the strength nor the opportunity to accomplish all the good and all the evil which we design.

~Marquis de Vauvenargues

We mustn't fear daylight just
because it almost always
illuminates a miserable world.

~René Magritte

Laws are like cobwebs, which
may catch small flies but let
wasps and hornets break
through.

~Jonathan Swift

GREATNESS

Great hopes make great men.

~Thomas Fuller

The world knows nothing of
its greatest men.

~Henry Taylor

He who walks in another's
tracks leaves no footprints.

~Joan L. Brannon

Greatness lies not in being
strong, but in the right use of
strength.

~Henry Ward Beecher

Ease and grace in everything.

~Baltasar Gracián

No great man ever complains
of want of opportunity.

~Ralph Waldo Emerson

No one looks at the blazing
sun; all do when it is eclipsed.

~Baltasar Gracián

He that seeketh to be eminent
amongst able men hath a great
task; but that is ever good for
the public. But he that plots to
be the only figure amongst
ciphers is the decay of a whole
age.

~Francis Bacon

The great man is he who has
not lost the heart of a child.

~Mencius

Always imitate the behavior of
the winners when you lose.

~George Meredith

Be not afraid of greatness:
some are born great; some

achieve greatness, and some
have greatness thrust upon
them.

~William Shakespeare

~

Mediocrity is a hand-rail.

~Charles Baron de
Montesquieu

Great men too make mistakes.

~Georg Christoph
Lichtenberg

Censure is the tax a man pays to
the public for being eminent.

~Jonathan Swift

Nothing so strong as gentleness,

Nothing is so gentle as real
strength.

~St. Francis de Sales

The great man is he that does
not lose his child's heart.

~Mencius

An occasional weakness in a
great man is a comfort to the
rest of us.

~Herbert Prochnow

No great man lives in vain. The
history of the world is but the
biography of great men.

~Thomas Carlyle

No man ever yet became great
by imitation.

~Samuel Johnson

Curiosity is, in great and
generous minds, the first
passion and the last.

~Samuel Johnson

Many people would be much
better if they would let
themselves be as good as they

really are. They seem to take
delight in making themselves
less.

~Mark Rutherford

HABITS

What one does, one becomes.

      ~Spanish Proverb

Chaos often breeds life, when order breeds habit.

      ~Henry Adams

~

We are shaped and fashioned
by what we love.

~Johann Wolfgang von
Goethe

Little and often fills the purse.

      ~German Proverb

A man too busy to take care of
his health is like a mechanic too
busy to take care of his tools.

      ~Spanish Proverb

HAPPINESS

We are no longer happy as
soon as we wish to be happier.

~Walter Savage Landor

True happiness ... is not
attained through self-
gratification, but through
fidelity to a worthy purpose.

~Helen Keller

If we only wanted to be happy,
it would be easy; but we want
to be happier than other
people, and that is almost
always difficult, since we think
them happier than they are.

~Charles Baron de
Montesquieu

The only way to avoid being
miserable is not to have
enough leisure to wonder
whether you are happy or not.

~George Bernard Shaw

~

Happiness or unhappiness is
made wholly to depend on the
quality of the object which we
love.

~Baruch Spinoza

The soul is the wife of the body.
They do have the same kind of
pleasure or, at least, they
seldom enjoy it at the same
time.

~Paul Valéry

Happiness and Beauty are by-
products.

~George Bernard Shaw

The best way for a man to lead
his life is to have been as
cheerful as possible and to have
suffered as little as possible.
This could happen if one did

not seek one's pleasures in
mortal things.

~Democritus of Abdera

The essence of philosophy is
that a man should so live that
his happiness shall depend as
little as possible on external
things.

~Epictetus

It is not easy to find happiness
in ourselves, and it is not
possible to find it elsewhere.

~Agnes Repplier

As we are always preparing to
be happy, it is inevitable that we
should never be so.

~Blaise Pascal

No one truly knows happiness
who has not suffered.

~Henri Frédéric Amiel

The poor man is happy; he
expects no change for the worse.

~Demetrius

No man is happy; he is at best
fortunate.

~Solon

To be able to fill leisure
intelligently is the last product
of civilization.

~Bertrand Russell

HOME

Without hearts there is no home.

> ~Lord Byron

He is happiest, be he king or peasant, who finds peace in his home.

> ~Johann Wolfgang von Goethe

No place is more delightful than one's own fireside.

> ~Cicero

But what on earth is half so dear – so longed for – as the hearth of home?

> ~Emily Bronte

Whom God loves, his house is sweet to him.

> ~Miguel de Cervantes

A comfortable home is a great source of happiness. It ranks immediately after health and a good conscience.

> ~Sydney Smith

The path of duty lies in what is near, and man seeks for it in what is remote.

> ~Mencius

HONOR

Avoid the person who has no honor, for if he esteems not honor, he esteems not virtue. And honor is the throne of integrity.

~Baltasar Gracián

Speak what is very good, do what is very honorable.

~Baltasar Gracián

But the honorable man does not forget who he is because of what others are.

~Baltasar Gracián

As you get older, it is harder to have heroes, but it is sort of necessary.

~Ernest Hemingway

Treat everyone as a gentleman; not because they are, but because you are.

~Ed Sabol

~

It is more difficult to be an honourable man for a week than to be a hero for fifteen minutes.

~Jules Renard

HOPE

Hope dies last but sickens first.

~Fulvio Fiori

The young are slaves to dreams.

~Theodore Roosevelt

It is only on those who hang on for ten minutes after all is hopeless, that hope begins to dawn.

~G.K. Chesterton

While there's life, there's hope.

~Terence

All human wisdom is summed up in two words – wait and hope.

~Alexandre Dumas

Hope springs eternal in the human breast.

~Alexander Pope

Another flower shall spring.

~William Blake

Everything one *records* contains a grain of hope, no matter how deeply it may come from despair.

~Elias Canetti

When we are flat on our back, there is no way to look but up.

~Roger Babson

Never despair. But if you do, work on in despair.

~D. Burke

We are all in the gutter, but some of us are looking at the stars.

~Oscar Wilde

The most absurd and the most rash hopes have sometimes been the cause of extraordinary success.

~Marquis de
Vauvenargues

Hope is itself a species of happiness and perhaps the chief happiness which this world affords.

~Samuel Johnson

Our hopes, often though they deceive us, lead us pleasantly along the path of life.

~François Duc de la
Rochefoucauld

Hope is generally a wrong guide, though it is very good company by the way.

~Lord Halifax

We should never let our fears hold us back from pursuing hopes.

~John F. Kennedy

~

Hope is nothing else but an inconstant pleasure,
Arising from the image of something future or past,
Whereof we do not yet know the issue.

Fear, on the other had, is an inconstant pain
Also arising from the image of something concerning
Which we are in doubt.

If the element of doubt be removed from these emotions,
Hope becomes confidence
And fear becomes despair.

~Baruch Spinoza

If you do not hope, you will not find what is beyond your hopes.

~St. Clement of
Alexandria

The most absurd and most rash
hopes have sometimes been the
cause of extraordinary success.

~Marquis
Vauvenargues

Hope is a good breakfast, but it
is a bad supper.

~Francis Bacon

Hope has a good memory,
gratitude a bad one.

~Baltasar Gracián

Vows begin when hope dies.

~Leonardo da Vinci

Hope awakens courage. He
who can implant courage in the
human soul is the best
physician.

~Karl Von Knebel

Walk on, walk on, with hope in
your heart; and you'll never
walk alone; you'll never walk
alone.

~Rodgers &
Hammerstein

He has gained enough who
gives up a vain hope.

~Italian Proverb

The natural flights of the human
mind are not from pleasure to
pleasure, but from hope to
hope.

~Samuel Johnson

The sudden disappointment of
a hope leaves a scar which the
ultimate fulfillment of that hope
never entirely removes.

~Thomas Hardy

There is one thing which gives
radiance to everything. It is the
idea of something around the
corner.

~G.K. Chesterton

Everything that is done in the world is done by hope.

~Martin Luther

HUMILITY

Loquacity storms the ear, but modesty takes the heart.

~Robert South

The only way to be loved is to be gentle and pleasant.

~Baltasar Gracián

~

Modesty is the only sure bait when you angle for praise.

~G.K. Chesterton

In humility the mind is at rest and peace; patience is her daughter.

~St. Francis of Assisi

The crown of a good disposition is humility.

~Arabian Proverb

Few men speak humbly of humility, chastely of chastity, skeptically of skepticism.

~Blaise Pascal

HUMOR

The world is a comedy to those who think and a tragedy to those who feel.

~Horace Walpole

Life is a tragedy for those who feel and a comedy for those who think.

~Jean de La Bruyère

My way of joking is telling the truth; that is the funniest joke in the world.

~George Bernard Shaw

He is a (sane) man who can have tragedy in his heart and comedy in his head.

~G.K. Chesterton

Jesters do oft prove prophets.

~William Shakespeare

Laughter is the habitual crying of the wise.

~Magdalena Samozwaniec

We must laugh at a man to avoid crying for him.

~Napoleon

~

Laugh, if thou art wise.

~Martial

Men show their characters in nothing more clearly than in what they think laughable.

~Johann Wolfgang von Goethe

Comedy is the last refuge of the non-conformist mind.

~George Seldes

What sunshine is to flowers, smiles are to humanity. They are but trifles to be sure; but, scattered along life's pathway, the good they do is inconceivable.

~Joseph Addison

The essence of humor is sensibility; warm tender fellow-feeling with all forms of existence.

~Thomas Carlyle

Joking and humor are pleasant, and often of extreme utility.

~Cicero

A good laugh is sunshine in a house.

~William Makepeace
Thackeray

A little nonsense, now and then, is relished by the wisest men.

~Anonymous

He is not laughed at who laughs at himself first.

~Anonymous

That day is lost on which one has not laughed.

~French Proverb

Comedy is simply a funny way of being serious.

~Peter Ustinov

One needs a dash of satire to enliven even a eulogy.

~Voltaire

IGNORANCE

Ignorance, the root and the stem of every evil.

~Plato

One learns by doing the thing; for though you think you know it, you have no certainty until you try.

~Sophocles

Nothing is more terrible than ignorance in action.

~Johann Wolfgang von Goethe

~

Ignorance cannot always be inferred from inaccuracy; knowledge is not always present.

~Samuel Johnson

Even supposing knowledge to be easily attainable, more people would be content to be ignorant than would take even a little trouble to acquire it.

~Samuel Johnson

There are many things of which a wise man might wish to be ignorant.

~Ralph Waldo Emerson

That man must be tremendously ignorant: he answers every question that is put to him.

~Voltaire

To be ignorant of one's ignorance is the malady of the ignorant.

~Bronson Alcott

A little learning is a dangerous thing.

~Alexander Pope

Prejudice is the reasoning of the stupid.

~Voltaire

Most men, when they think they are thinking, are merely rearranging their prejudices.

~Knute Rockne

O God, help us not to despise or oppose what we do not understand.

~William Penn

INDIVIDUALISM

**You can tell the ideals of a
nation by its advertisements.**

~Douglas Norman

~

However indifferent men are to
universal truths, they are keen
on those that are individual and
particular.

~Arthur Schopenhauer

The most universal quality is
diversity.

~Michel de Montaigne

There is no such thing as human
perfection.

~D.H. Lawrence

The eagle never lost so much
time as when he submitted to
learn of the crow.

~William Blake

Most people are other people.
Their thoughts are someone
else's opinions, their lives a
mimicry, their passions a
quotation.

~Oscar Wilde

There is much of mankind that a
man can learn only from
himself.

~Walter Bagehot

How glorious it is and how
pointed to be an exception.

~Alfred de Musset

INTEGRITY

To conquer without nobility is
not victory but surrender.

~Baltasar Gracián

You should be able to boast
that if gallantry, generosity,
and faith were lost in the
world, they could be found
again in your own breast.

~Baltasar Gracián

He may fall into error, but he
doesn't lie down and make his
home there.

~Baltasar Gracián

For a noble person, there is
nothing more expensive than
what is given to him free.

~Baltasar Gracián

Words demonstrate integrity,
and deeds even more so.

~Baltasar Gracián

Try to be heroic rather than
merely seem so.

~Baltasar Gracián

A man who looks after his
actions sees that others see
him, or will.

~Baltasar Gracián

He knows that walls have ears,
and that what is badly done is
bursting to become known.

~Baltasar Gracián

~

Waste no more time arguing
what a good man should be. Be
one.

~Marcus Aurelius

It is usurping life to do no more than simply avoid doing harm; the dead do as much, and exact nothing for it.

~Prince de Ligne

Men of business must not break their word twice.

~Thomas Fuller

Though a good deal is too strange to be believed, nothing is too strange to have great men.

~Thomas Hardy

With malice toward none, with charity for all.

~Abraham Lincoln

Character builds slowly, but it can be torn down again with incredible swiftness.

~Faith Baldwin

Men of character are the conscience of the society to which they belong.

~Ralph Waldo Emerson

JEALOUSY

The silence of the envious is too noisy.

> ~Kahlil Gibran

~

A jealous man always finds more than he is looking for.

> ~Madeleine de Scudéry

Envy which talks and cries out is always maladroit; it is the envy which keeps silent that one ought to fear.

> ~Antoine de Rivarol

One of envy's favourite stratagems is the attempt to provoke envy in the envied one.

> ~Leslie Farber

The gilded sheath of pity conceals the dagger of envy.

~Friedrich Nietzsche

Oh what a bitter thing it is to look into happiness through another man's eyes.

> ~William Shakespeare

Man will do many things to get himself loved; he will do all things to get himself envied.

> ~Mark Twain

Envy lurks at the bottom of the human heart like a viper in its hole.

> ~ Honoré de Balzac

In jealousy there is more self-love than love.

> ~François Duc de la Rochefoucauld

Jealousy is nothing more than the fear of abandonment.

~Anonymous

Lots of people know a good
thing the minute the other
fellow sees it first.

~Job Hedges

JOY

It is a great art to know how to enjoy all good things.

   ~Baltasar Gracián

To live much and to take pleasure in life is to live twice.

   ~Baltasar Gracián

It is useful to know exactly how to enjoy each person.

   ~Baltasar Gracián

Joy is a fruit that Americans eat green.

   ~Armando Zegri

Most sorts of diversion in men, children, and other animals, are an imitation of fighting.

   ~Jonathan Swift

~

Most men pursue pleasure with such breathless haste that they hurry past it.

   ~ Søren Kierkegaard

All animals except man know that the ultimate in life is to enjoy it.

   ~Samuel Butler

Mere life is not a blessing, but to live well.

   ~Seneca

JUDGMENT

The more you judge, the less you love.

~Honoré de Balzac

Only those who aren't hungry are able to judge the quality of a meal.

~Alessandro Morandotti

Take no content in the ills of others, and don't comment on them.

~Baltasar Gracián

Many smash the mirror that reminds them of their ugliness.

~Baltasar Gracián

He that would live in peace and ease

Must not speak all he knows nor judge all he sees.

~Benjamin Franklin

Do not judge, or you too will be judged.

~Jesus Christ

He alone is an acute observer who can observe minutely without being observed.

~Johann Kaspar Lavater

~

If we escape punishment for our vices, why should we complain if we are not rewarded for our virtues?

~Churton Collins

Wink at small faults; for thou has great ones.

~Thomas Fuller

There may be said to be two classes of people in the world: those who constantly divide the people of the world into two classes, and those who do not.

~Robert Benchley

You will not become a saint through other people's sins.

~Anton Chekhov

I hear very much of people's calling out to punish the guilty, but very few are concerned to clear the innocent.

~Daniel Defoe

Let me be a little kinder,

Let me be a little blinder

To the faults of those around me.

~Edgar A. Guest

One can advise comfortably from a safe port.

~Friedrich Schiller

If thou art a master, be sometimes blind, if a servant, sometimes deaf.

~Thomas Fuller

Let us leave … labels to those who have little else where-with to cover their nakedness.

~Walter Sickert

Behind man acts that are thought ridiculous there lie wise and weighty motives.

~ François Duc de la Rochefoucauld

The more intelligent a man is, the more originality he discovers in men. Ordinary people see no difference between men.

~Blaise Pascal

KINDNESS

We expect to pass through this world but once. Any good we can do, therefore, or any kindness that we can show to any fellow creature, let us do it now; let us not defer or neglect it, for we shall not pass this way again.

~Stephen Grellet

A loving heart is the truest wisdom.

~Charles Dickens

That best portion of a good man's life,

His little, nameless, unremembered acts,

Of kindness and of love.

~William Wordsworth

Forget injuries; never forget kindness.

~Confucius

Kindness in words creates confidence. Kindness in thinking creates profoundness. Kindness in giving creates love.

~Lao-Tse

Civility costs nothing and buys everything.

~Lady Mary Wortley Montagu

Let charm and courtesy capture the goodwill of others.

~Baltasar Gracián

~

If you have it (charm), you don't need to have anything else, and if you don't have it, it doesn't much matter what else you have.

100

~James M. Barrie

A man with a sour face should not open a shop.

~Japanese Proverb

Do not wait for extraordinary circumstances to do good; try to use ordinary situations.

~Jean Paul Richter

Kindness – a language which the dumb can speak, and the deaf can understand.

~Christian Bovee

Kindness is the golden chain by which society is bound together.

~Voltaire

I love thee for a heart that's kind,

Not for the knowledge of thy mind.

~W.H. Davies

To cultivate kindness is a valuable part of the business of life.

~Samuel Johnson

Kind hearts are more than coronets.

~Alfred Lord Tennyson

Wise sayings often fall on barren ground, but a kind word is never thrown away.

~Sir Arthur Helps

If a man be gracious, and courteous to strangers, it shows he is a citizen of the world...

~Francis Bacon

KNOWLEDGE

In much wisdom is much grief:
and he that increaseth
knowledge increaseth sorrow.

> ~Ecclesiastes

Simple ideas lie within the
reach only of complex minds.

> ~Remy de Gourmont

What you don't understand,
you don't possess.

> ~Johann Wolfgang von
> Goethe

He that knows little often
repeats it.

> ~Thomas Fuller

You really know when you
know little; doubt grows with
knowledge.

> ~Johann Wolfgang von
> Goethe

One who is content just to
experience life and act
accordingly has all the truth he
needs. This is the wisdom of
the growing child.

> ~Johann Wolfgang von
> Goethe

Nothing is the world except
health and virtue is more to be
treasured than knowledge and
learning; nor is anything so
easily attainable and so cheap
to acquire: all you have to do is
to be still, all you have to
spend is time, something we
cannot save in any other way
then by spending it.

> ~Johann Wolfgang von
> Goethe

We have little to live and much
to know, and you cannot live if
you do not know.

> ~Baltasar Gracián

One of the greatest gifts is to seize up quickly what matters.

~Baltasar Gracián

There are occasions where the greatest knowledge lies in appearing to have none.

~Baltasar Gracián

Wisdom matters little to fools, and madmen care little for sanity. So speak to everyone in his own tongue.

~Baltasar Gracián

To be admired by others, wear the hide of an ass.

~Baltasar Gracián

He is a hard man who is only just, and a sad one who is only wise.

~Voltaire

Those who cannot remember the past are condemned to repeat it.

~George Santayana

Knowledge is power.

~Francis Bacon

~

The ink of the scholar is more holy than the blood of the martyr.

~Muhammad

Acquire knowledge. It enables its possessor to distinguish right from wrong; it lights the way to heaven; it is our friend in the desert, our society in solitude, our companion when friendless; it guides us to happiness; it sustains us in misery; it is an ornament among friends, and an armor against enemies.

~Muhammad

A man who studies wisdom,
even insincerely, should be
called wise.

~Yoshida Kenkō

Uncultivated minds are not full
of wild flowers, like
uncultivated fields. Villainous
weeds grow in them, and they
are full of toads.

~Logan Pearsall Smith

Whether learning has made
more proud men or good men,
may be a question.

~Anonymous

Knowledge without sense is
double folly.

~ Baltasar Gracián

The three primary principles of
wisdom: obedience to the laws
of God, concern for the welfare
of mankind, and suffering with
fortitude all the accidents of life.

~Anonymous

If a man could have half his
wishes, he would double his
troubles.

~Benjamin Franklin

Everybody loves the tree which
gives him shelter.

~Russian Proverb

Wisdom thoroughly learned
will never be forgotten.

~Pythagoras

Wisdom is to the soul what
health is to the body.

~De Saint-Réal

You cannot gauge the
intelligence of an American by
talking with him.

~Eric Hoffer

Knowledge is capable of being
its own end.

~John Henry Cardinal
Newman

Seeking to know is only too
often learning to doubt.

~Deshoulières

Crafty men condemn studies,
simple men admire them, and
wise men use them.

~Francis Bacon

Knowledge is little; to know the
right context is much; to know
the right spot is everything.

~Hugo von
Hofmannsthal

By suffering comes wisdom.

~Aeschylus

It is not enough to have a good
mind. The main thing is to use
it well.

~René Descartes

LEADERSHIP

They seize the respect, the heart, and even the minds of others.

~Baltasar Gracián

Ideals travel upward, manners downward.

~Edward Bulwer-Lytton

Imitation is the sincerest form of flattery.

~Charles Caleb Colton

~

The greatest carver does the least cutting.

~Lao-tse

Great evils befall the world when the powerful begin to copy the weak. The desperate devices which enable the weak to survive are unequaled instruments of oppression and extermination in the hands of the strong.

~Eric Hoffer

So much of what we call management consists of making it difficult for people to work.

~Peter Drucker

LEARNING & TEACHING

We receive three educations, one from our parents, one from our schoolmasters, and one from the world. The third contradicts all that the first two teach us.

~Charles Baron de
Montesquieu

Ye can lade a man up to th'university, but ye can't make him think.

~Finley Peter Dunne

To teach is to learn twice.

~Joseph Joubert

Scholars are men of peace, they bear no arms, but their tongues are sharper than Actius his razor, their pens carry farther and give a louder report than thunder; I had rather stand in the shock of a basilica [a large cannon] than in the fury of a merciless pen.

~Sir Thomas Browne

Knowledge rests not upon truth alone, but upon error also.

~Carl Jung

~

Who is wise? He who learns from all men, as it is said, From all my teachers have I gotten understanding.

~Simeon Ben Zoma

The self-educated are marked by stubborn peculiarities.

~Isaac D'Israeli

Experience is a good teacher, but she sends in terrific bills.

~Minna Antrim

Expect poison from the standing water.

~William Blake

Our ignorance of history makes us libel to our own times. People have always been like this.

~Gustave Flaubert
(1821~1880)

In giving advice, I advise you, be short.

~Horace

I have found the best way to give advice to your children is to find out what they want and then advise them to do it.

~Harry Truman

Prejudice is the child of ignorance.

~William Hazlitt

If a man's education is finished, he is finished.

~Edward Filene

A moment's insight is sometimes worth a life's experience.

~Oliver Wendell
Holmes

At a certain age, some people's minds close up. They live on their intellectual fat.

~William Lyon Phelps

The man who is too old to learn was probably always too old to learn.

~Henry Haskins

I am always ready to learn although I do not always like being taught.

~Winston Churchill

In doing we learn.

~George Herbert

Learning makes a good man better and an ill man worse.

~Thomas Fuller

I pay the schoolmaster but tis the schoolboys that educate my son.

~Ralph Waldo Emerson

I have learned silence from the talkative, toleration from the intolerant, and kindness from the unkind; yet strange, I am ungrateful to those teachers.

~Kahlil Gilbran

Those who are slow to know suppose that slowness is the essence of knowledge.

~Friedrich Nietzsche

Doctrine should be such as should make men in love with the lesson and not with the teacher.

~Francis Bacon

The world, where much is to be done and little to be known.

~Samuel Johnson

Youth is a blunder; manhood a struggle; old age a regret.

~Benjamin Disraeli

One repays a teacher badly if one always remains nothing but a pupil.

~Friedrich Nietzsche

How is it possible to expect that mankind will take advice, when they will not so much as take warning.

~Jonathan Swift

A man who has committed a mistake and doesn't correct it is committing another mistake.

~Confucius   Mistakes are their own
instructors.

~Horace

LIFE

Life is a warfare against the malice of others.

~Baltasar Gracián

Everything that lives is Holy.

~William Blake

Although many die of foolishness, few fools ever really die, for few ever begin to live.

~Baltasar Gracián

Life must be lived forwards, but can only be understood backwards.

~Søren Kierkegaard

May you live all the days of your life.

~Jonathan Swift

Only a life lived for others is a life worthwhile.

~Albert Einstein

Life is as tedious as a twice-told tale, vexing the dull ear of a drowsy man.

~William Shakespeare

~

Everything is worthy of notice, for everything can be interpreted.

~Hermann Hesse

Is life worth living? This is a question for an embryo, not for a man.

~Samuel Butler

Life is like playing a violin solo in public and learning the instrument as one goes on.

111

~Samuel Butler

Life is an offensive, directed against the repetitious mechanism of the universe.

~Alfred North Whitehead

There is no cure for birth or death save to enjoy the interval.

~George Santayana

If God adds another day to our life, let us receive it gladly.

~Marcus Annaeus Seneca

The average man who does not know what to do with his life wants another one which will last forever.

~Anatole France

The world either breaks or hardens the heart.

~Nicolas Chamfort

I slept and dreamed that life was beauty,

I woke – and found that life was duty.

~Ellen Sturgis Hooper

Life's but a walking shadow, a poor player

That struts and frets his hour upon the stage

And then is heard no more; it is a tale

Told by an idiot, full of sound and fury,

Signifying nothing

~William Shakespeare

If life is a grind, use it to sharpen your wits.

~Anonymous

I have seen all the works that are done under the sun; and behold, all is vanity and vexation of spirit.

~Solomon

LOVE

Perhaps a great love is never returned.

~Dag Hammarskjöld

L'amour est un vrai recommenceur.

(Love is truly a new beginning).

~Johann Wolfgang von Goethe

He who doesn't see his lover's faults as virtues is not in love.

~Johann Wolfgang von Goethe

Nothing is sadder than to watch the absolute urge for the unconditional in this altogether conditional world.

~Johann Wolfgang von Goethe

Love takes more liberties than hatred.

~Baltasar Gracián

True love is like seeing ghosts: we all talk about it, but few of us have ever seen one.

~ François Duc de la Rochefoucauld

In love, there is always one who kisses and one who offers the cheek.

~French proverb

The magic of first love is our ignorance that it can ever end.

~Benjamin Disraeli

They do not love that do not show their love.

~William Shakespeare

The course of true love never did run smooth.

~William Shakespeare

There is a road from the eye to the heart that does not go through the intellect.

~G.K. Chesterton

~

This being in love is great – you get a lot of compliments and begin to think that you are a great guy.

~F. Scott Fitzgerald

Love, like fire, cannot survive without continual movement, and it ceases to live as soon as it ceases to hope or fear.

~François Duc de la Rochefoucauld

There are two kinds of faithfulness in love: one is based on forever finding new things to love in the loved one; the other

is based on our pride in being faithful.

~François Duc de la Rochefoucauld

What is irritating about love is that it is a crime that requires an accomplice.

~Charles Baudelaire

Love, as it is practiced in society, is merely the exchange of two momentary desires and the contact of two skins.

~Sébastien-Roch Nicolas De Chamfort

No one has ever loved anyone the way everyone wants to be loved.

~Mignon McLaughlin

Love knows hidden paths.

~Anonymous

To be loved, be lovable.

~Ovid

But there's nothing half so
sweet in life

As love's young dream

~Thomas Moore

Love is love's reward.

~John Dryden

Will you love me in the good
old fashioned way?

When my hair has all turned
gray,

Will you kiss me then and say,

That you love me in December
as you do in May?

~James J. Walker

Love and dignity cannot share
the same abode.

~Ovid

Love, and a cough, cannot be
hid.

~George Herbert

To know her was to love her.

~Samuel Rogers

All mankind love a lover.

~Ralph Waldo Emerson

The creative mind plays with
the objects it loves.

~Carl Gustav Jung

LUCK

Leave your luck while still winning.

> ~Baltasar Gracián

Chance never helps those who do not help themselves.

> ~Sophocles

A wise man turns chance into good fortune.

> ~Thomas Fuller

> ~

There is no one luckier than he who thinks himself so.

> ~German Proverb

Fortune, seeing that she could not make fools wise, has made them lucky.

> ~Michel de Montaigne

Diligence is the mother of good fortune.

> ~Miguel de Cervantes

MANKIND

It is easier to know man in general than to understand one man in particular.

~François Duc de la
Rochefoucauld

Civilization has rendered man, if not more bloodthirsty, at least a worse (in the sense of a meaner) thirstier after blood than before.

~Fyodor Dostoevsky

Most humans beings have an almost infinite capacity for taking things for granted.

~Aldous Huxley

Man spends his life in reasoning on the past, in complaining of the present, in fearing for the future.

~Antoine Rivarol

Man is the only animal who causes pain to others with no other object than wanting to do so.

~Arthur Schopenhauer

A man has generally the good or ill qualities which he attributes to mankind.

~William Shenstone

Man is a make-believe animal – he is never so truly himself as when he is acting a part.

~William Hazlitt

We do not learn to know men through their coming to us. To find out what sort of persons they are, we must go to them.

~Johann Wolfgang von
Goethe

If you pick up a starving dog and make him prosperous, he will not bite you. That is the principal difference between a dog and a man.

~Mark Twain

MARRIAGE

Soul meets soul on lover's lips.

~Percy Bysshe Shelley

~

If you marry for money, you will earn every penny.

~Dr. Phil McGraw

An intelligent woman is a woman with whom one can be as stupid as one wants.

~Paul Valéry

All tragedies are finish'd by a death,

All comedies are ended by a marriage.

~Lord Byron

Love is blind, but marriage restores its sights.

~Georg Christoph Lichtenberg

When one feels oneself smitten by love for a woman, one should say to oneself, 'Who are the people around her, What kind of life has she led?' All one's future happiness lies in the answer.

~Alfred de Vigny

It is a mistake for a taciturn, serious-minded woman to marry a jovial man, but not for a serious-minded man to marry a lighthearted woman.

~Johann Wolfgang von Goethe

Better to sit up all night, than to go bed with a dragon.

~Jeremy Taylor

Unmarried men very rarely
speak the truth about the things
that most nearly concern them;
married men, never.

~Samuel Butler

Marriage has many pains, but
celibacy no pleasures.

~Samuel Johnson

To marry a second time
represents the triumph of hope
over experience.

~Samuel Johnson

Grow old along with me!
The best is yet to be…

~Robert Browning

If you go to war pray once; if
you go on a sea journey pray
twice; but pray three times
when you are going to be
married.

~Russian Proverb

He knows little who will tell his
wife all he knows.

~Thomas Fuller

There are few women so perfect
that their husbands do not
regret having married them at
least once a day.

~Jean de La Bruyère

To take a wife merely as an
agreeable and rational
companion will commonly be
found to be a grand mistake.

~Lord Chesterfield

Bachelors know more about
women than married men. If
they didn't they'd be married
too.

~H.L. Mencken

Call no man unhappy until he's
married.

~Socrates

A bachelor never quite gets over the idea that he is a thing of beauty and a boy forever.

~H. Rowland

MODERATION

The hardest thing is to take
less when you can get more.

~Frank McKinney
Hubbard

Moderation in all things.

~Terence

Gluttony is an emotional
escape, a sign that something is
eating us.

~Peter de Vries

Foolishness always deals in
excess.

~Baltasar Gracián

All sunshine makes a desert.

~Arabian Proverb

~

A wise man sees as much as he
ought, not as much as he can.

~ Michel de Montaigne

A wise man will live as much
within his wit as his income.

~Earl of Chesterfield

123

MOMENTS & MEMORY

This – this was what made life: a moment of quiet, the water falling in the fountain, the girl's voice ... <u>a moment of captured beauty</u>. He who is truly wise will never permit such moments to escape.

> ~Louis L'Amour

We do not remember the days, we remember the moments.

> ~Cesare Pavese

God gave us memory that we might have roses in December.

> ~Sir James M. Barrie

~

Where interest lags, memory lags too.

> ~Johann Wolfgang von Goethe

MONEY

The price we pay for money is paid in liberty.

~Robert Louis Stevenson

That which we give makes us richer, that which is hoarded is lost.

~Shota Rustaveli

A man is wealthy in proportion to the things he can do without.

~Epicurus

Fortune does not change men; it unmasks them.

~Madame Necker

You will only achieve (riches) in one way, by convincing yourself that you can live a happy life even without them, and by always regarding them as being on the point of vanishing.

~Seneca

Wealth is not his who has it, but his who enjoys it.

~Benjamin Franklin

The rich are indeed rather possessed by their money than possessors.

~Robert Burton

~

The lack of money is the root of all evil.

~Mark Twain

Is it only the mouth and belly which are injured by hunger and thirst? Men's minds are also injured by them.

~Mencius

If you want to know what a man is really like, take notice how he acts when he loses money.

~New England proverb

Great riches have sold more men than they have bought.

~Francis Bacon

The best condition in life is not to be so rich as to be envied nor as poor as to be damned.

~Josh Billings

Never run into debt, not if you can find anything else to run into.

~Josh Billings

Cleanse thy heart from greed, and thy foot shall remain free from fetters.

~Arabian Proverb

The riches that are in the heart cannot be stolen.

~Russian Proverb

A man often pays dearly for a small frugality.

~Ralph Waldo Emerson

Those who know when they have enough are rich.

~Chinese Proverb

It's good to have money and the things that money can buy but it's good to check up once in a while to make sure you haven't lost the things that money can't buy.

~George Claude Lorimer

The love of money is the mother of all evil.

~Phocylides

The seven deadly sins… Food, clothing, firing, rent, taxes, respectability and children. Nothing can lift those seven millstones from man's neck but money; and the spirit cannot soar until the millstones are lifted.

~George Bernard Shaw

The way to enrich are many, and most of them foul.

~Francis Bacon

A rich man is nothing but a poor man with money.

~W.C. Fields

I have not observed men's honesty to increase with their riches.

~Thomas Jefferson

Money is a sweet balm.

~Arab Proverb

No man ever had enough money.

~Gypsy Proverb

Make money, money by fair means if you can, if not, by any means money.

~Horace

One must be poor to know the luxury of giving.

~George Eliot

Wealth by which some people think to get a reputation, does but expose the more their weaknesses and follies

~Anonymous

To be clever enough to get all that money, one must be stupid enough to want it.

~G.K. Chesterton

There is nothing so habit-forming as money.

~Don Marquis

Plenty of people despise money, but few know how to give it away.

~François Duc de la Rochefoucauld

This love of place, and precedency, it rocks us in our cradles, it lies down with us in our graves.

~John Donne

Poverty is the openmouthed relentless hell which yawns beneath civilized society.

~Henry George

Poverty is a great enemy to human happiness.

~Samuel Johnson

To be poor and independent is very nearly an impossibility.

~William Cobbett

MOTIVATION

Nobody is bored when he is trying to make something that is beautiful or to discover something that is true.

~Ralph William Inge

Could we know what men are most apt to remember, we might know what they are most apt to do.

~Marquis of Halifax

~

Taken as a whole, men will only devote their enthusiasm, their time, and their energy to matters in which their passions have a personal interest. But their personal interests, however powerful they may be, will never carry them very far or very high unless they can be made to seem noble and legitimate in their own eyes by being allied to some great cause in which the whole human race can join.

~Alexis de Tocqueville

Inequality is the cause of all local movements.

~Leonardo da Vinci

Every man is a revolutionist concerning the thing he understands.

~George Bernard Shaw

Young fellows are tempted by girls; men who are thirty years old are tempted by gold; when they are forty years old, they are tempted by honor and glory, and those who are sixty years old, say to themselves, 'What a pious man I have become.'

~Martin Luther

The reasonable man adapts himself to the world; the unreasonable one persists in trying to adapt the world to himself. Therefore all progress depends on the unreasonable man.

~George Bernard Shaw

NOVELTY

A brand-new mediocrity is
more highly regarded than an
extremely talented person to
whom we have grown
accustomed.

~Baltasar Gracián

Remember that the glory of
novelty lasts little.

~Baltasar Gracián

In these new towns, one can
find the old houses only in
people.

~Emanuel Canete

~

When a thing ceases to be a
subject of controversy, it ceases
to be a subject of interest.

~William Hazlitt

OLD AGE

The young man knows the rules, but the old man knows the exceptions.

~Oliver Wendell Holmes

~

Old people are fond of giving advice; it consoles them for no longer being capable of setting a bad example.

~François Duc de la Rochefoucauld

Extremely happy and extremely unhappy men are alike prone to grow hardhearted.

~Baron de La Brede Montesquieu

For the unlearned, old age is winter; for the learned it is the season of the harvest.

~Talmud

Old age takes away from us what we have inherited and gives us what we have earned.

~Gerald Brenan

Men are like wine; some turn to vinegar, but the best improve with age.

~Pope John XXIII

The thorns which I have reaped are of the tree I planted.

~Lord Byron

OPPORTUNITIES

Next to knowing when to seize an opportunity, the most important thing in life is to know when to forgo an advantage.

~Benjamin Disraeli

Opportunities multiply as they are seized; they die when neglected. Life is a long line of opportunities.

~John Wicker

I think luck is the sense to recognize an opportunity and the ability to take advantage of it. Everyone has bad breaks, but everyone also has opportunities. The man who can smile at his breaks and grab his chances gets on.

~Samuel Goldwyn

We must look for the opportunity in every difficulty

instead of being paralyzed at the thought of the difficulty in every opportunity.

~Walter E. Cole

The opportunity is often lost by deliberating.

~Publilius Syrus

Luck affects everything. Let your hook always be cast in the stream where you least expect there will be fish.

~Ovid

~

A wise man will make more opportunities than he finds.

~Francis Bacon

The people who get on in this world are the people who get up and look for the circumstances they want, and, if they can't find them, make them.

~George Bernard Shaw

My hat is in the ring.

~Theodore Roosevelt

Ability is nothing without opportunity.

~Napoleon

Enthusiasm finds the opportunities, and energy makes the most of them.

~Henry Hoskins

Much will have more.

~Ralph Waldo Emerson

Wealth in modern societies is distributed according to opportunity; and while opportunity depends partly upon talent and energy, it depends still more upon birth, social position, access to education and inherited wealth; in a word, upon property.

~Richard H. Tawney

PARENTING

Like father, like son.

~William Langland

Greatness of name in the father oft-times overwhelms the son; they stand too near one another. The shadow kills the growth: so much, that we see the grandchild come more and oftener to be heir of the first.

~Ben Jonson

The best academy, a mother's knee.

~James Russell Lowell

The hand that rocks the cradle is the hand that rules the world.

~William Ross Wallace

PASSION & ENERGY

From a little spark may burst a mighty flame.

~Dante Alighieri

~

Men's passions are so many roads by which they can be reached.

~Marquis Vauvenargues

His passions make man live, his wisdom merely makes him last.

~Sébastien-Roch Nicolas De Chamfort

When you have found out the prevailing passion of any man, remember never to trust him where that passion is concerned.

~G.K. Chesterton

He that would be superior to external influences must first become superior to his own passions.

~Samuel Johnson

There is no fire like passion, there is no shark like hatred, there is no snare like folly, there is no torrent like greed.

~Buddha

It is harder to hide feelings we have than to feign those we lack.

~François Duc de la Rochefoucauld

Passion and prejudice govern the world.

~John Wesley

Energy is eternal delight.

~Marquis de Vauvenargues

PATIENCE

The most important rule for living lies in knowing how to bear all things.

> ~Baltasar Gracián

Enjoy the blessings of this day, if God sends them; and the evils of it bear patiently and sweetly; for this day only is ours; we are dead to yesterday, and we are not yet born to the morrow.

> ~Jeremy Taylor

Patience is bitter, but its fruit sweet.

> ~Jean Jacques Rousseau

Patience, and shuffle the cards.

> ~Miguel de Cervantes

Learn to labour and to wait.

> ~Henry Wadsworth Longfellow

~

There is nothing which human courage will not undertake, and little that human patience will not endure.

> ~Samuel Johnson

The test of good manners is to be patient with bad ones.

> ~Solomon Ibn Gabirol

Patience is a most necessary quality for business: many a man would rather you heard his story than granted his request.

> ~Earl of Chesterfield

Have patience with all things, but chiefly have patience with yourself. Do not lose courage in considering your own imperfections, but instantly set about remedying them – every day begin the task anew.

~Saint Francis de Sales

He that can have patience can have what he will.

~Benjamin Franklin

Genius is eternal patience.

~Michelangelo

God's love for poor sinners is very wonderful, but God's patience with ill-natured saints is a deeper mystery.

~Henry Drummond

Endeavor to be patient in bearing the defects and infirmities of others, of what sort soever they be; for thou thyself also hast many failings which must be borne with by others.

~Thomas à Kempis

Let joy, temperance and repose

Slam the door on the doctor's nose.

~Henry Wadsworth Longfellow

Patience, the beggar's virtue.

~Philip Massinger

PERFECTION

Perfection does not exist. To understand this is the triumph of human intelligence; to expect to possess it is the most dangerous kind of madness.

~Alfred de Musset

There is no perfection in humanity.

~Samuel Montagne

A man would do nothing if he waited until he could do it so well that no one could find fault.

~John Henry Cardinal Newman

Perfectionism is a dangerous state of mind in an imperfect world.

~Robert Hillyer

Perfectionism is slow death.

~Hugh Prather

The man who makes no mistakes lacks boldness and the spirit of adventure. He never tries anything new. He is a brake on the wheels of progress.

~M.W. Larmour

Have patience with all things, but chiefly have patience with yourself. Do not lose courage in considering your own imperfections, but instantly set about remedying them – every day begin the task anew.

~Saint Francis de Sales

He who has the understanding to declare his limitations is closest to perfection.

~Johann Wolfgang von Goethe

Perfection isn't quantity, but quality.

~Baltasar Gracián

~

A confusion of the real with the ideal never goes unpunished.

~Johann Wolfgang von Goethe

Every man who refuses to accept the conditions of life sells his soul.

~Charles Baudelaire

PERSEVERANCE

I am not concerned that you
have fallen; I am concerned
that you arise.

> ~Abraham Lincoln

When you feel how
depressingly

Slowly you climb,

It's well to remember that

Things Take Time.

> ~Piet Hein

Much rain wears the marble.

> ~William Shakespeare

With ordinary talent and
extraordinary perseverance, all
things are attainable.

> ~Sir Thomas Foxwell
> Buxton

Life begins on the other side of
despair.

> ~Jean-Paul Sartre

Effort only fully releases its
reward after a person refuses to
quit.

> ~Napoleon Hill

I'm a little wounded, but I am
not slain; I will lay me down to
bleed a while. Then I'll rise
and fight again.

> ~John Dryden

Our greatest glory consists not
in never falling, but in rising
every time we fall.

> ~Ralph Waldo Emerson

Cling tooth and nail to the
following rule: not to give in to
adversity, never to trust
prosperity, and always take
full note of fortune's habit of
behaving just as she pleases,

treating her as if she were actually going to do everything it is in her power to do. Whatever you have been expecting for some time comes as less of a shock.

~Seneca

Advancing years bring greater trials.

~Johann Wolfgang von Goethe

Know how to get things done: it may not be the highest thing in life, but it is the most necessary.

~Baltasar Gracián

What is worth doing is worth finishing.

~Baltasar Gracián

I will write of him who fights and vanquishes his sins, who struggles on through weary

years against himself ... and wins.

~Caroline Begelow LeRow

Ad astra per ardua.

(To the stars through difficulties).

~Ralph Waldo Emerson

Any idiot can face a crisis ~ it's this day-to-day living that wears you out.

~Anton Chekhov

To endure is greater than to dare; to tire out hostile fortune; to be daunted by no difficulty; to keep heart when all have lost it ~ who can say this is not greatness?

~William Makepeace Thackeray

The art of life is to know how to enjoy a little and to endure much.

~William Hazlitt

That which is bitter to endure may be sweet to remember.

~Thomas Fuller

Know how sublime a thing is To suffer and be strong.

~Henry Wadsworth Longfellow

~

He conquers who endures.

~Italian Proverb

Not everything that is more difficult is more meritorious.

~Saint Thomas Aquinas

Hitch your wagon to a star.

~Ralph Waldo Emerson

Motivation is what gets you started. Habit is what keeps you going.

~Jim Ryuh

A hero is one who knows how to hang on one minute longer.

~Anonymous

The greatest man is he who chooses the right with the most invincible resolution; who resists the sorest temptation from within and without; who bears the heaviest burden cheerfully; who is calmest in storms, and most fearless under menaces and frowns; whose reliance on truth, on virtue, and on God is most unfaltering.

~Seneca

~Benjamin Franklin

Great minds have purposes;
others have wishes. Little
minds are tamed and subdued
by misfortunes, but great minds
rise above them.

~Washington Irving

Many men owe the grandeur of
their lives to their tremendous
difficulties.

~Charles Haddon
Spurgeon

Great people are not affected by
each puff of wind that blows ill.
Like great ships, they sail
serenely on, in a calm sea or a
great tempest.

~George Washington

The business of life is to go
forwards.

~Samuel Johnson

Little strokes fell great oaks.

Courage and perseverance have
a magical talisman, before
which difficulties disappear and
obstacles vanish into air.

~John Quincy Adams

The longest day will have an
end.

~Anonymous

No pain, no palm;

No thorns, no throne;

No gall, no glory;

No cross, no crown.

~William Penn

To suffer and to endure is the
lot of humanity.

~Pope Leo XIII

Man cannot remake himself
without suffering. For he is
both the marble and the
sculptor.

~Alexis Carrel

PESSIMISM

Some complain of past
offenses and give rise to future
ones.

~Baltasar Gracián

The prudent person should
never publicize dishonor or
slights, only the esteem others
have shown him.

~Baltasar Gracián

~

He who seeks happiness for
himself by making others
unhappy is bound in the chains
of hate and from those he
cannot be free.

~*The Dhammapada*

Wretches are ungrateful; it is
part of their wretchedness.

~Victor Hugo

Those see nothing but faults
that seek for nothing else.

~Thomas Fuller

There are people who have an
appetite for grief; pleasure is not
strong enough and they crave
pain.

~Ralph Waldo Emerson

The malicious have a dark
happiness.

~Victor Hugo

Keep away from people who try
to belittle your ambitions. Small
people always do that, but the
really great make you feel that
you, too, can become great.

~Mark Twain

A loving person lives in a loving
world. A hostile person lives in

a hostile world. Everyone you
meet is your mirror.

~Ken Keyes Jr.

PLANNING

Any plan is bad which is not
susceptible to change.

~Italian Proverb

One must lose a minnow to
catch a salmon.

~French Proverb

The chameleon does not leave
one tree until he is sure of
another.

~Arabian Proverb

Thatch your roof before rainy
weather; dig your well before
you become parched with thirst.

~Chinese Proverb

PLEASURE

There is no such thing as pure pleasure; some anxiety always goes with it.

~Ovid

Pleasure is the absence of pain.

~Cicero

Pleasure is nothing else but the intermission of pain.

~John Selden

~

He who rides the tiger is afraid to dismount.

~Chinese Proverb

He who only lives wise lives a sad life.

~Voltaire

Pleasure is very seldom found where it is sought.

~Samuel Johnson

POLITICS

You ask which form of
government is best?
Whichever teaches us to govern
ourselves.

~Johann Wolfgang von
Goethe

It is hard to come to terms with
the errors of the times: if you
oppose them, you stand alone;
if you allow yourself to be
caught up in them, you get
neither honour nor joy in the
process.

~Johann Wolfgang von
Goethe

'Whoever wants to deceive
people must first of all make
absurdity plausible.'

~Johann Wolfgang von
Goethe

~

There are no small steps in great
affairs.

~Cardinal Jean Francois
de Retz

O Freedom, what liberties are
taken in thy name.

~Daniel George

Servitude debases men to the
point where they end up liking
it.

~Marquis
Vauvenargues

Extreme hopes are born of
extreme misery.

~Bertrand Russell

It is a general error to imagine
the loudest complainers for the
public to be the most anxious
for its welfare.

~Edmund Burke

Power will intoxicate the best hearts, as wine the strongest heads.

~Charles Caleb Colton

Wars begin when you will, but they do not end when you please.

~Niccolò Machiavelli

The weakness of all Utopias is this, that they take the greatest difficulty of man and assume it can be overcome, and then give an elaborate account of the overcoming of the smaller ones.

~G.K. Chesterton

Is life so dear, or peace so sweet, as to be purchased at the price of chains and slavery? Forbid it, Almighty God! I know not what course others take, but as for me, give me liberty or give me death!

~Patrick Henry

It is not best to swap horses while crossing the river.

~Abraham Lincoln

Politics makes strange bedfellows.

~Charles Dudley Warner

Blessed are the young for they shall inherit the national debt.

~Herbert Hoover

Democracy gives every man the right to be his own oppressor.

~John Lowell

Democracy substitutes election by the incompetent many for appointment by the corrupt few.

~George Bernard Shaw

Democracy consists of choosing your dictators after they've told

you what you think it is you
want to hear.

~Arnold Coven

Diplomacy is the art of letting
someone have your way.

~Daniele Vare

A Liberal is a man who will give
away everything he doesn't
own.

~F. Dane

A Liberal is a man too
broadminded to take his own
side in a quarrel.

~Barry Goldwater

The God who gave us life gave
us liberty at the same time.

~Thomas Jefferson

They that give up essential
liberty to obtain a little
temporary safety deserve
neither liberty no safety.

~Benjamin Franklin

In politics there is no honour.

~Benjamin Disraeli

Politics. The conduct of public
affairs for private advantage.

~Ambrose Bierce

Television in its present form…
is the opiate of the people of the
United States.

~Richard Nixon

POSITIVE THINKING

Some people are always
grumbling because roses have
thorns. I am thankful that
thorns have roses.

~Alphonse Karr

What a man thinks of himself,
that is what determines, rather
indicates, his fate.

~Henry David Thoreau

To find and to appreciate
goodness everywhere is the
sign of a love of truth.

~Johann Wolfgang von
Goethe

~

The American people never
carry an umbrella. They
prepare to walk in eternal
sunshine.

~Al Smith

What a man thinks of himself,
that is what determines, or
rather indicates his fate.

~Henry David Thoreau

As a man is, so he sees.

~William Blake

The cistern contains: the
fountain overflows.

~William Blake

Where everything is bad it must
be good to know the worst.

~Francis Herbert
Bradley

To look up and not down,

To look forward and not back,

To look out and not in, and

To lend a hand.

~Edward Everett Hale

The world is moving so fast these days that the man who says it can't be done is generally interrupted by someone doing it.

~Elbert Hubbard

A man must not complain of his "element," or of his "time," or the like; it is thriftless work doing so. His time is bad; well then, he is there to make it better.

~Thomas Carlyle

A man's being in a good or bad humor depends upon his will.

~Samuel Johnson

POSSESSION

To have everything one must
give everything.

~Augusto Roa Bastos

What you've hidden is lost.
What you've given away is all
yours.

~Shota Rustaveli

There are many things that we
would throw away, if we were
not afraid that others might
pick them up.

~Oscar Wilde

~

To own nothing is the
beginning of happiness.

~Diogenes

Do not regard as valuable
anything that can be taken
away.

~Seneca

You can't get rid of what really
belongs to you, even if you
throw it away.

~Johann Wolfgang von
Goethe

In order to possess, one must
first have desired.

~Marcel Proust

He that has satisfied his thirst
turns his back on the well.

~Baltasar Gracián

If all were possession, all
would be disappointment and
discontent.

~Baltasar Gracián

POWER

The secret of any power is this: to know that others are even more cowardly than we are.

~Ludwig Borne

The only advantage of having power is that you can do greater good.

~Baltasar Gracián

~

Power tends to corrupt and absolute power corrupts absolutely.

~Lord Acton

They who are in highest places, and have the most power, have the least liberty, because they are most observed.

~John Tillotson

Power, like lightning, injures before its warning.

~Calderon

Power is always gradually stealing away from the many to the few, because the few are more vigilant and consistent.

~Samuel Johnson

The only prize much cared for by the powerful is power.

~Oliver Wendell Holmes, Jr.

The lust for power, for dominating others, inflames the heart more than any other passion.

~Tacitus

Power, like a desolating pestilence,

Pollutes whate'er it touches...

~Percy Bysshe Shelley

PRAISE & BLAME

When everyone praises you
your funeral has begun.

~Julien de Valckenaere

Don't find fault, find a remedy.

~Henry Ford

It takes less courage to be the
only one to find fault than to
be the only one to find favor.

~Marie von Ebner-
Eschenbach

Great tranquility of heart is his
who cares for neither praise
nor blame.

~Thomas à Kempis

The applause of a single
human being is of great
consequence.

~Samuel Johnson

Fear of hypocrites and fools is
the great plague of thinking
and writing.

~Jules Gabriel Janin

The refusal of praise is a wish
to be praised twice.

~François Duc de la
Rochefoucauld

~

What is the sign of a proud
man? He never praises anyone.

~The Zohar

You must not pay a person a
compliment, and then
straightway follow it with a
criticism.

~Mark Twain

Caricature is the tribute that
mediocrity pays to genius.

~Oscar Wilde

Praises to the unworthy are felt
by the ardent minds as
robberies of the deserving.

~Samuel Taylor
Coleridge

Faint Praise is Disparagement.

~Thomas Fuller

REACTIONS

I love the man that can smile in
trouble, that can gather
strength from distress, and
grow brave by reflection.

~Thomas Paine

Don't curse the darkness –
light a candle.

~Chinese proverb

~

Ah, how ghastly is a hurt from
one whom you daren't
complain!

~Publilius Syrus

REALITY

Reality never catches up to imagination.

> ~Baltasar Gracián

~

One's real life is so often the life that one does not lead.

> ~Oscar Wilde

One real world is enough.

> ~George Santayana

Repetition is reality, and it is the seriousness of life.

> ~Søren Kierkegaard

The mind that renounces once and forever a futile hope has its compensation in ever-growing calm.

> ~George Gissing

Real life is, to most men, a long second-best, a perpetual compromise between the ideal and the possible.

> ~Bertrand Russell

RELIGION

'Tis not the dying for a faith that's so hard; 'tis the living up to it that is difficult.

~William Makepeace Thackeray

~

The union of skepticism and yearning begets mysticism.

~Friedrich Nietzsche

The scriptures teach us the best way of living, the noblest way of suffering, and the most comfortable way of dying.

~John Flavel

Nobody ever outgrows scripture; the book widens and deepens with our years.

~Charles Spurgeon

I like the silent church before the service begins, better than any preaching.

~Ralph Waldo Emerson

If a man have a strong faith he can indulge in the luxury of skepticism.

~Friedrich Nietzsche

We dream much of paradise, or rather of a number of successive paradises, but each of them is, long before we die, a paradise lost, in which we should feel ourselves lost too.

~Marcel Proust

Many might go to heaven with half the labour they go to hell.

~Ben Jonson

RESPONSIBILITY

No snowflake in an avalanche
ever feels responsible.

> ~ Stanisław Jerzy Lec

In the end, we will remember
not the words of our enemies
but the silence of our friends.

> ~Martin Luther King Jr.

What one has, one ought to
use; and whatever he does, he
should do with all his might.

> ~Cicero

He turns not back who is
bound to a star.

> ~Leonardo da Vinci

~

To put the world in order we
must first put the nation in
order.

To put the nation in order we
must first put the family in
order.

To put the family in order we
must first cultivate our personal
life.

And to cultivate our personal
life, we must set our hearts
right.

> ~Confucius

He who is good for making
excuses is seldom good for
anything else.

> ~Benjamin Franklin

RISK

To laugh is to risk appearing
the fool.

To weep is to risk appearing
sentimental.

To reach for another is to risk
involvement.

To expose your ideas, your
dreams, before a crowd, is to
risk their loss.

To love is to risk not being
loved in return.

To live is to risk dying.

To believe is to risk failure.

But risks must be taken,
because the greatest hazard in
life is to risk nothing.

The people who risk nothing
do nothing, have nothing, are
nothing.

They may avoid suffering and
sorrow, but they cannot learn,
feel, change, grow, love, live.

Chained by their attitudes,
they are slaves; they have
forfeited their freedom.

Only a person who risks is
free.

~Anonymous

Only those who dare to fail
greatly can ever achieve
greatly.

~Robert F. Kennedy

For all sad words of tongue or
pen the saddest are these: 'It
might have been!'

~John Greenleaf
Whittier

Be wary of the man who urges
an action in which he himself
incurs no risk.

~Joaquin Setanti

Who dares nothing, need hope
for nothing.

~J.C.F. von Schiller

164

Many things are lost for want of asking.

~English proverb

Most of the time things are not obtained because they were not attempted.

~Baltasar Gracián

Monotony is the awful reward of the careful.

~A.G. Buckham

~

The secret for harvesting from existence the greatest fruitfulness and the greatest enjoyment is ~ to live dangerously!

~Friedrich Nietzsche

Those who'll play with cats must expect to be scratched.

~Miguel de Cervantes

Asking costs little.

~Italian Proverb

Only those those who will risk going too far can possibly find out how far one can go.

~T.S. Eliot

Risk is what separates the good part of life from the tedium.

~J. Zero

There is no such thing as absolute certainty, but there is assurance sufficient for the purposes of human life.

~John Stuart Mill

As you grow older, you'll find the only things you regret are the things you didn't do.

~Zachary Scott

ROUGH DAYS

'Tis healthy to be sick
sometimes.

> ~Henry David Thoreau

If matters go badly now, they
will not always be so.

> ~Horace

The only law that does not
change is that everything
changes, and the hardship I was
bearing today was only a breath
away from the pleasures I
would have tomorrow, and
those pleasures would be all the
richer because of the memories
of this I was enduring.

> ~Louis L'Amour

Life comes in clusters, clusters
of solitude, then clusters when
there is hardly time to breathe.

> ~May Sarton

RULERS

None climb so high as he who
knows not whither he is going.

~Oliver Cromwell

How many weak shoulders
have craved heavy burdens!

~Joseph Joubert

Great men, like great cities,
have many crooked arts, and
dark alleys in their hearts,
whereby he that knows them
may save himself much time
and trouble.

~Charles Caleb Colton

The civilities of the great are
never thrown away.

~Samuel Johnson

A great man does enough for us
when he refrains from doing us
harm.

~Pierre de
Beaumarchais

People who have power
respond simply. They have no
minds but their own.

~Ivy Compton-Burnett

SECRECY

What was silent in the father speaks in the son; and often I found in the son the unveiled secret of the father.

~Friedrich Nietzsche

~

There is more of fear than delight in a secret pleasure.

~Publilius Syrus

Explaining is generally half confessing.

~Marquess of Halifax

There is something about a cupboard that makes a skeleton terribly restless.

~Anonymous

Never let the bottom of your purse or your mind be seen.

~Anonymous

SELF-ACCEPTANCE

No one can make you feel inferior without your consent.

~Eleanor Roosevelt

It is the chiefest point of happiness that a man is willing to be what he is.

~Erasmus

It is better to be hated for what you are than loved for what you are not.

~Andre Gide

All is disgust when one leaves his own nature and does things that misfit it.

~Sophocles

~

It is the greatest of all inconsistencies to wish to be other than we are.

~Arthur Schopenhauer

If God wanted me otherwise, He would have created me otherwise.

~Johann Wolfgang von Goethe

Resolve to be thyself … he who finds himself loses his misery!

~Matthew Arnold

If you make friends with yourself you will never be alone.

~Maxwell Maltz

Nothing is a greater impediment to being on good terms with others than being ill at ease with yourself.

169

~Honoré de Balzac

Let us humbly accept from God
even our own nature, and treat
it charitably, firmly,
intelligently. Not that we are
called upon to accept the evil
and disease in us, but let us
accept *ourselves* in spite of the
evil and the disease.

~Henri-Frédéric Amie

Be patient with everyone, but
above all with yourself. I mean,
do not be disturbed because of
your imperfections, and always
rise up bravely from a fall.

~St. Francis de Sales

What part soever you have
taken upon you, play that as
well as you can and make the
best of it.

~Sir Thomas More

SELF-CONFIDENCE

As soon as you trust yourself,
you will know how to live.

~Johann Wolfgang von
Goethe

Confidence is contagious. So
is lack of confidence.

~Vince Lombardi

The wind cannot shake a
mountain. Neither praise nor
blame moves the wise man.
Happiness or sorrow -
whatever befalls you, walk on
untouched, unattached.

~Buddha

Don't be made of glass in your
dealings with others.

~Baltasar Gracián

Pay no attention to what they
say, and less to what they feel.

~Baltasar Gracián

It is always the secure who are
humble.

~Gilbert Keith
Chesterton

Trust thyself; every heart
vibrates to that iron string.

~Ralph Waldo Emerson

~

Insist on yourself; never imitate.

~Ralph Waldo Emerson

Whatever the world may say or
do, my part is to remain an
emerald and keep my colour
true.

~Marcus Aurelius

A timid question will always
receive a confident answer.

~Mr. Justice Darling

~Cicero

Every man stamps his value on himself... man is made great or small by his own will.

~J.C.F. von Schiller

The confidence which we have in ourselves gives birth to much of that which we have in others.

~François Duc de la Rochefoucauld

Every man has a right to be conceited until he is successful.

~Benjamin Disraeli

Never bend your head. Always hold it high. Look the world straight in the face.

~Helen Keller

Too many people overvalue what they are not and undervalue what they are.

~Malcolm Forbes

People do not lack strength; they lack will.

~Victor Hugo

Confidence is that feeling by which the mind embarks on great and honorable courses with a sure hope and trust in itself.

Self-confidence is the first requisite to great undertakings.

~Samuel Johnson

SELF-CONTROL

Be master of your will and servant of your conscience.

~Marie Von Ebner-Eschenbach

There is little that can withstand a man who can conquer himself.

~Louis XIV

No mastery is greater than mastering yourself and your own passions: it is a triumph of the will.

~Baltasar Gracián

Master yourself and you will master others.

~Baltasar Gracián

~

The educated man tries to repress the inferior one in himself, without realizing that by this he forces the latter to become revolutionary.

~Carl Gustav Jung

I count him braver who overcomes his desires than him who conquers his enemies; the hardest victory is the victory over self.

~Aristotle

There is a luxury in self-reproach. When we blame ourselves, we feel no one else has a right to blame us.

~Oscar Wilde

Most powerful is he who has himself in his own power.

~Seneca

173

SELF-DOUBT

The contemplative life is often miserable. One must act more, think less, and not watch oneself live.

> ~Sébastien-Roch
> Nicolas De Chamfort

~

Wrongs are often forgiven, but contempt never is. Our pride remembers it for ever.

> ~Lord Chesterfield

It is easier to cope with a bad conscience than with a bad reputation.

> ~Friedrich Nietzsche

We recognize that flattery is poison, but its perfume intoxicates us.

> ~Marquis de la Grange

Sometimes we think we dislike flattery, but it is only the way it is done that we dislike.

> ~François Duc de la
> Rochefoucauld

When we ask advice we are usually looking for an accomplice.

> ~Marquis de la Grange

When we feel that we lack whatever is needed to secure someone else's esteem, we are very close to hating him.

> ~Marquis
> Vauvenargues

Ridicule often checks what is absurd, and fully as often smothers that which is noble.

> ~Sir Walter Scott

A great deal of talent is lost to the world for the want of a little courage.

~Sydney Smith

No one likes to be pitied for his faults.

~Marquis
Vauvenargues

To show pity is felt as a sign of contempt because one has clearly ceased to be an object *fear* as soon as one is pitied.

~Friedrich Nietzsche

What is best about a great victory is that it liberates the victor from the fear of defeat.

~Friedrich Nietzsche

When men are easy in themselves, they let others remain so.

~Lord Shaftesbury

The excessive desire of pleasing goes along almost always with the apprehension of not being liked.

~Thomas Fuller

Jealousy is the great exaggerator.

~Friedrich von Schiller

Hide not your talents, for use they were made; what's a sun-dial in the shade?

~Benjamin Franklin

SELF-IDENTITY

The accent of one's birthplace persists in the mind and heart as much as in speech.

~François Duc de la Rochefoucauld

~

As a rule a man's face says more of interest that does his tongue.

~Arthur Schopenhauer

The voice is a second face.

~Gerard Bauer

One of the unpardonable sins, in the eyes of most people, is for a man to go about <u>unlabelled</u>. The world regards such a person as the police do an unmuzzled dog, not under proper control.

~T.H. Huxley

SELF-KNOWLEDGE

We know what we are, but not
what we may be.

~William Shakespeare

Almost every man wastes part
of his life in attempts to
display qualities which he
does not possess, and to gain
applause which he cannot
keep.

~Samuel Johnson

Self-correction begins with
self-knowledge.

~Baltasar Gracián

You cannot master yourself if
you do not understand
yourself.

~Baltasar Gracián

It is a luxury to be understood.

~Ralph Waldo Emerson

At thirty a man should know
himself like the palm of his
hand, know the exact number
of his defects and qualities ...
And above all, accept these
things.

~Albert Camus

~

Consciousness of our strength
increases it.

~Marquis de Vauvenargues

Up to a certain point every man
is what he thinks he is.

~F.H. Bradley

Any one is to be pitied who has
just sense enough to perceive
his deficiencies.

~William Hazlitt

It is not impossibilities which
fill us with the deepest despair,
but possibilities which we have
failed to realize.

~Robert Mallet

We cannot disengage ourselves
from what we condemn.

~Michel de Montaigne

The innocent are so few that
two of them seldom meet –
when they do meet, their
victims lie strewn all around.

~Elizabeth Bowen

A stumble may prevent a fall.

~Thomas Fuller

People seem not to see that their
opinion of the world is also a
confession of character.

~Ralph Waldo Emerson

It is one thing to praise
discipline, and another to
submit to it.

~Miguel de Cervantes

Not all those who know their
minds know their hearts as
well.

~ François Duc de la
Rochefoucauld

Almost all absurdity of conduct
arises from the imitation of
those whom we cannot
resemble.

~Samuel Johnson

Until we lose ourselves, there is
no hope of finding ourselves.

~Henry Miller

No one knows what he can do
till he tries.

~Latin Proverb

Know thyself.

~Anonymous

Keep pace with the drummer
you hear, however measured or
far away.

~Henry David Thoreau

SELF-LOVE

As you treat your body, so your house, your domestics, your enemies, your friends – dress is a table of your contents.

~Johann Kaspar Lavater

Vanity is other people's pride.

~Sacha Guitry

To love oneself is the beginning of a lifelong romance.

~François Duc de la Rochefoucauld

~Oscar Wilde

There are many things we despise in order that we may not have to despise ourselves.

~Marquis Vauvenargues

Esteem yourself if you want esteem from others.

~Baltasar Gracián

The most important thing is to be whatever you are without shame.

~Rod Steiger

~

Self-love is love of oneself and of all things in terms of oneself; it makes men worshippers of themselves and would make them tyrants over others if fortune gave them the means.

~François Duc de la Rochefoucauld

He that considers how little he dwells upon the conditions of others will learn how little the attention of others is attracted by himself.

~Samuel Johnson

We are more anxious to speak
than to be heard.

~Henry Thoreau

To others we are not ourselves
but a performer in their lives
cast for a part we do not even
know that we are playing.

~Elizabeth Bibesco

Self-love is subtler than the
subtlest man in the world.

~François Duc de la
Rochefoucauld

Vanity dies hard; in some
obstinate cases it outlives the
man.

~Robert Louis
Stevenson

To love oneself is the beginning
of a life-long romance.

~Oscar Wilde

Men sometimes feel injured by
praise because it assigns a limit
to their merit.

~Marquis
Vauvenargues

We are so vain that we even
care for the opinion of those we
don't care for.

~Maria von Ebner-
Eschenbach

We all think we are exceptional,
and are surprised to find
ourselves criticized just like
anyone else.

~Comtesse Diane

One is vain by nature, modest
by necessity.

~Pierre Reverdy

Conceit is the finest armour a
man can wear.

~Jerome K. Jerome

He that overvalues himself will undervalue others, and he that undervalues others will oppress them.

~Samuel Johnson

We measure the excellency of other men, by some excellency we conceive to be in ourselves.

~John Selden

We are so presumptuous that we think we can separate our personal interest from that of humanity, and slander mankind without compromising ourselves.

~Marquis Vauvenargues

Nobody hates a proud man more than a proud man.

~Anonymous

Self-love rightly defined is far from being a fault. A man who loveth himself right will do everything else right.

~Marquess of Halifax

You can never get rid of what is part of you, even if you throw it away.

~Johann Wolfgang von Goethe

Perhaps one should not think so much of oneself, though it is an interesting subject.

~Norman Douglas

We hate the thing we fear, the thing we know may be true and may be true and may have a certain affinity with ourselves, for each man hates himself.

~Cesare Pavese

I cannot love anyone if I hate myself.

~Carl Gustav Jung

Consistency requires you to be as ignorant today as you were a year ago.

~Bernard Berenson

We refuse praise from a desire to be praised twice.

~ François Duc de la Rochefoucauld

There is overwhelming evidence that the higher the level of self-esteem, the more likely one will treat others with respect kindness, and generosity. People who do not experience self-love have little or no capacity to love others.

~Nathaniel Branden

Healthy personalities accept themselves not in any self-idolizing way, but in the sense that they see themselves as persons who are worth giving to another and worthy to receive from another.

~William Klassen

The fundamental problem most patients have is an inability to love themselves, having been unloved by others during some crucial part of their lives.

~Bernie S. Siegel, M.D.

Flattery is counterfeit money which, but for vanity, would have no circulation.

~François Duc de la Rochefoucauld

Self-preservation is the first law of nature.

~Samuel Butler

What makes the vanity of other people insupportable is that it wounds our own.

~François Duc de la Rochefoucauld

One will rarely err if extreme actions be ascribed to vanity,

ordinary actions to habit, and
mean actions to fear.

~Friedrich Nietzsche

Make the most of yourself, for
that is all there is to you.

~Ralph Waldo Emerson

SELF-RELIANCE

He who knows how to suffer everything can dare everything.

~Marquis de Vauvenargues

The wise are sufficient unto themselves.

~Baltasar Gracián

Trust your heart, especially when it is a strong one.

~Baltasar Gracián

~

Be lamps unto yourselves.

~Buddha

Self-sufficiency is the greatest of all wealth.

~Epicurus

You should aim to be independent of any one vote, of any one fashion, of any one century.

~Baltasar Gracián

Men are never attached to you by favors.

~Napoleon Bonaparte

Self-distrust is the cause of most of our failures … they are the weakest, however strong, who have no faith in themselves or their own powers.

~Christian Bovee

The best place to find a helping hand is at the end of your own arm.

~Swedish proverb

The man who makes everything that leads to happiness depend

on himself, and not upon other
men, has adopted the very best
plan for living happily.

~Plato

SELF-RESTRAINT

It is in self-limitation that a master first shows himself.

> ~Johann Wolfgang von Goethe

You can have everything if you care little for what matters nothing.

> ~Baltasar Gracián

~

Good manners are made up of petty sacrifices.

> ~Ralph Waldo Emerson

It is always safe to assume that people are more subtle and less sensitive than they seem.

> ~Eric Hoffer

Never esteem anything as of advantage to thee that shall make thee break thy word or lose thy self-respect.

> ~Marcus Aurelius

SELFISHNESS

Selfishness is not living as one wishes to live. It is asking others to live as one wishes to live.

~Oscar Wilde

Despair is the absolute extreme of self-love. It is reached when a man deliberately turns his back on all help from anyone else in order to taste the rotten luxury of knowing himself to be lost.

~Thomas Merton

~

The worst cliques are those which consist of one man.

~George Bernard Shaw

He was like a cock who thought the sun had risen to hear him crow.

~George Eliot

Conceit is God's gift to little men.

~Bruce Barton

188

SHREWDNESS

The best way to keep one's word is not to give it.

~Napoleon Bonaparte

A wise man will keep his suspicions muzzled, but he will keep them awake.

~Marquess of Halifax

~

The shortest and best way to make your fortune is to let people see clearly that it is in their interests to promote yours.

~Jean de La Bruyère

Knowledge, sense, honesty, learning, good behaviour are the chief things towards making a man's fortune, next to interest and opportunity.

~Anonymous

The clever man often worries; the loyal person is often overworked.

~'Mr. Tut-Tut'

The reason why fools and knaves thrive better in the world than wiser and honester men is because they are nearer to the general temper of mankind.

~Samuel Butler (I)

The path of social advancement is, and must be, strewn with broken friendships.

~H.G. Wells

A man has made great progress in cunning when he does not seem too clever to others.

~Jean de La Bruyère

Never tell your resolutions beforehand.

~John Selden

The greatest of all secrets is knowing how to reduce the force of envy.

~Cardinal Jean Francois de Retz

If you wish to win a man's heart, allow him to confute you.

~Benjamin Disraeli

Yield to a man's tastes and he will yield to your interests.

~Edward Bulwer-Lytton

Birds are taken with pipes that imitate their own voices, and men with those sayings that are most agreeable to their own opinions.

~Samuel Butler

What really flatters a man is that you think him worth flattering.

~George Bernard Shaw

SIMPLICITY

Clearness is the ornament of deep thought.

~Marquis de Vauvenargues

It is a great boldness to dare to simplify oneself.

~Marie-Joesphine de Suin de Beausacq

Simplicity is the ultimate sophistication.

~Leonardo da Vinci

Fear less, hope more;

Eat less chew more;

Whine less, breathe more;

Talk less, say more;

Love more, and all good things will be yours.

~Swedish proverb

The wisdom of life consists in the elimination of nonessentials.

~Lin Yutang

Simple pleasures are the last refuge of the complex.

~Oscar Wilde

~

Simplicity of character is no hindrance to subtlety of intellect.

~John Morley

Manifest plainness,

Embrace simplicity,

Reduce selfishness,

Have few desires.

~Lao-tse

There is no greatness where there is not simplicity.

~Leo Tolstoy

Simplicity, carried to an extreme, becomes elegance.

~Joe Franklin

The greatest truths are the simplest, and so are the greatest men.

~Julius Charles Hare

Simplicity of character is the natural result of profound thought.

~William Hazlitt

Have nothing in your house that you do not know to be useful or believe to be beautiful.

~William Morris

The little things are what is eternal, and the rest, all the rest, is brevity, extreme brevity.

~Antonio Porchia

By a tranquil mind, I mean nothing else than a mind well ordered.

~Marcus Aurelius

SOCIETY

Be prepared. For the rude, the stubborn, the vain, and for all sorts of fools.

> ~Baltasar Gracián

A slave has but one master; an ambitious man has as many masters as there are people who may be useful in bettering his position.

> ~Jean de La Bruyère

~

Society,
Which is called the world,
Is nothing but the contention of
a thousand clashing petty
interests,
An eternal conflict of all the
vanities that cross each other,
Strike against each other,
Are wounded and humiliated
by each other in turn,
And expiate on the morrow,
In the bitterness of defeat,
The triumph of the day before.

To live alone,
To avoid the bruises of
wretched scrapes
In which one attracts all eyes
one minute
Only to be trampled on the next,
Is to be what they call nothing,
To have no existence.

Poor humanity!

> ~Sébastien-Roch Nicolas Chamfort

People who cannot bear to be alone are generally the worst company.

> ~Albert Guinon

To be happy, we must not be too concerned with others.

> ~Albert Camus

No man can have society upon his terms. If he seeks it, he must serve it too.

~Ralph Waldo Emerson

The moment you enter society, you draw the key from your heart and put it in your pocket. Those who fail to do so are fools.

~Johann Wolfgang von Goethe

If you wish to become a philosopher you must not be disheartened by the first distressing discoveries you make in your study of human beings.

~ Sébastien-Roch Nicolas Chamfort

It is the fools and the knaves that make the wheels of the World turn. They are the World; those few who have sense or honesty sneak up and down single, but never go in herds.

~Marquess of Halifax

You may break your heart, but men will still go on as before.

~Marcus Aurelius

The need for society which springs from the emptiness and monotony of men's lives drives them together; but their many unpleasant and repulsive qualities once more drive them apart. The mean distance which they finally discover, and which enables them to endure being together, is politeness.

~Arthur Schopenhauer

There is no need to visit a madhouse to find lunatics.

~Johann Wolfgang von Goethe

Manners… a contrivance of wise men to keep fools at a distance.

~Ralph Waldo Emerson

194

~Anatole France

Taxes are what we pay for
civilized society.

> ~Oliver Wendell
> Holmes, Jr.

In this world nothing is certain
but death and taxes.

> ~Benjamin Franklin

It is the folly of too many to
mistake the echo of a London
coffee-house for the voice of the
kingdom.

> ~Jonathan Swift

Of all the preposterous
assumptions of humanity over
humanity, nothing exceeds most
of the criticisms made on the
habits of the poor by the well-
housed, well-warmed, and well-
fed.

> ~Herman Melville

It is only the poor who are
forbidden to beg.

Thieves respect property. They
merely wish the property to
become their property that they
may more perfectly respect it.

> ~G.K. Chesterton

To be feared is to fear: no one
has been able to strike terror
into others and at the same time
enjoy peace of mind himself.

> ~Seneca

No grand idea was ever born in
a conference, but lots of foolish
ideas have died there.

> ~F. Scott Fitzgerald

Happy is the man who is hated
on his own account.

> ~Jean Rostand

Seek to be in harmony with all
your neighbors; live in amity
with your brethren.

195

~Confucius

SOLITUDE & ALONENESS

The lonely form the biggest group.

~Frans Hiddema

To live is to feel oneself lost.

~José Ortega y Gasset

All men's misfortune's spring from their hatred of being alone.

~Jean de La Bruyère

To be adult is to be alone.

~Jean Rostand

Solitude: A good place to visit, but a poor place to stay.

~Josh Billings

~

It is easy in the world to live after the world's opinion;
It is easy in solitude to live after our own;
But the great man is he who in the midst of the crowd keeps with perfect sweetness the independence of solitude.

~Ralph Waldo Emerson

Light is half a companion.

~Genoese proverb

He who does not enjoy solitude will not love freedom.

~ Arthur Schopenhauer

One can acquire everything in solitude except character.

~Henri Beyle Stendhal

If you are afraid of loneliness, don't marry.

~Anton Chekhov

Better to be alone than in bad company.

~Anonymous

Man cannot long survive without air, water, and sleep. Next in importance comes food. And close on its heels, solitude.

~Thomas Szasz

Whoever is delighted in solitude is either a wild beast or a god.

~Francis Bacon

A man alone, is either a saint or a devil.

~Robert Burton

Who can enjoy alone?

~John Milton

It is not good that the man should be alone…

~God

The worst loneliness is not to be comfortable with yourself.

~Mark Twain

Loneliness… is and always has been the central and inevitable experience of every man.

~Thomas Wolfe

Loneliness is the first thing which God's eye nam'd not good.

~John Milton

I wandered lonely as a cloud…

~William Wordsworth

SORROW & GRIEF

He is a (sane) man who can have tragedy in his heart and comedy in his head.

~G.K. Chesterton

A really intelligent man feels what other men only know.

~Baron de Montesquieu

There is a joy in sorrow which none but a mourner can know.

~Jean Paul Richter

Boredom is simply the lack of imagination.

~Julie O. Smith

Sorrow is a fruit. God does not allow it to grow on a branch that is too weak to bear it.

~Victor Hugo

Joy and sorrow are next door neighbors.

~German Proverb

This is my last message to you: in sorrow seek happiness.

~Feodor Dostoevsky

Sorrows are like thunderclouds. Far off they look black, but directly over us merely gray.

~Jean Paul Richter

Some natural sorrow, loss, or pain,

That has been, and may be again.

~William Wordsworth

~

I have often been forced to my knees by the overwhelming conviction that there was no place else to go.

~Abraham Lincoln

Sorrow concealed, like an oven stopp'd,

Doth burn the heart to cinders where it is.

~William Shakespeare

There is hardly any grief that an hour's reading will not dissipate.

~Charles Baron de Montesquieu

Come what may, time and the hour runs through the roughest day.

~William Shakespeare

Sadness flies on the wings of the morning, and out of the heart of darkness comes the light.

~Jean Giraudoux

Human misery must somewhere have a stop; there is no wind that always blows a storm.

~Euripides

Pain is never permanent.

~Saint Teresa of Avila

One day in retrospect the years of struggle will strike you as the most beautiful.

~Sigmund Freud

Wounds heal and become scars, but scars grow with us.

~Stanislaw Lec

Nothing is so soon forgot as pain. The moment it is gone the whole agony is over, and the thought of it can no longer give us any sort of disturbance.

~Adam Smith

How disappointment tracks the steps of hope.

~L. London

The heart's affections are divided like the branches of the cedar tree; if the tree loses one strong branch, it will suffer but it does not die. It will pour all its vitality into the next branch so that it will grow and fill the empty space.

~Kahlil Gibran

Laugh, and the world laughs with you;

Weep, and you weep alone.

~Ella Wheeler Wilcox

And if I laugh at any mortal thing,

'Tis that I may not weep.

~Lord Byron

There is so much to laugh at in this vale of tears.

~Suderman

Man is the only animal that laughs and weeps; for he is the only animal that is struck with the difference between what things are, and what they ought to be.

William Hazlitt

Boredom is the most horrible of wolves.

~John Giorno

SUCCESS

Be of good cheer. Do not think of today's failures, but of the success that may come tomorrow. You have set yourselves a difficult task, but you will succeed if you persevere; and you will find a joy in overcoming obstacles. Remember, no effort that we make to attain something beautiful is ever lost.

~Helen Keller

How can they say that my life is not a success? Have I not for more than sixty years got enough to eat and escaped being eaten?

~Logan Pearsall Smith

Success covers a multitude of blunders.

~George Bernard Shaw

The secret to success in life is for a man to be ready for his opportunity when it comes.

~Benjamin Disraeli

~

Success is relative: It is what we can make of the mess we have made of things.

~T.S. Eliot

Success or failure lies in conformity to the times.

~Niccolò Machiavelli

I have always observed that to succeed in the world one should seem a fool, but be wise.

~Baron de Montesquieu

Success has ruined many a man.

~Benjamin Franklin

The toughest thing about success is that you've got to keep on being a success. Talent is only a starting point in this business.

~Irving Berlin

SUSPICIONS & CONSPIRACIES

A wise man will keep his
suspicions muzzled, but he
will keep them awake.

> ~Marquess of Halifax

Irrationally held truths may be
more harmful than reasoned
errors.

> ~T.H. Huxley

Excusing yourself beforehand
awakens suspicions that were
fast asleep.

> ~Baltasar Gracián

Beware of telling an
improbable truth.

> ~Thomas Fuller

The cleverly expressed
opposite of any generally
accepted idea is worth a
fortune to somebody.

> ~F. Scott Fitzgerald

~

He who says there is no such
thing as an honest man, you
may be sure is himself a knave.

> ~Bishop Berkeley

To accuse requires less
eloquence (such is man's
nature) than to excuse.

> ~Hobbes

A striking expression, with the
aid of a small amount of truth,
can surprise us into accepting a
falsehood.

> ~Marquis
> Vauvenargues

There are infinite possibilities of
error, and more cranks take up
unfashionable untruths than
unfashionable truths.

~Bertrand Russell

There is nothing that makes a man suspect much, more than to know little.

~Francis Bacon

The best qualification of a prophet is to have a good memory.

~Marquess of Halifax

Suspicion is rather a virtue than a fault, as long as it doth like a dog that watched, and doth not bite.

~ Marquis of Halifax

There is no rule more invariable than that we are paid for our suspicions by finding what we suspected.

~Henry David Thoreau

I see men ordinarily more eager to discover a reason for things than to find out whether the things are so.

~Michel de Montaigne

A man does not look behind a door unless he has stood there himself.

~Henri Du Bois

Persistent prophecy is a familiar way of assuring the event.

~George Gissing

The crisis of today is the joke of tomorrow.

~H.G. Wells

If we believe absurdities, we shall commit atrocities.

~Voltaire

One dog yelping at nothing will set ten thousand straining at their collars.

~Japanese Proverb

Every cloud engenders not a storm.

~William Shakespeare

Impotent hatred is the most horrid of all emotions; one should hate nobody whom one cannot destroy.

~Johann Wolfgang von Goethe

SYMPATHIES

Men of cold passions have quick eyes.

~Nathaniel Hawthorne

To refrain from imitation is the best revenge.

~Marcus Aurelius

All the while thou studiest revenge, thou art tearing thy wound open.

~Thomas Fuller

A man that studieth revenge keeps his own wounds green.

~Francis Bacon

Some people are moulded by their admirations; others by their hostilities.

~Elizabeth Bowen

We spend our time envying people whom we wouldn't wish to be.

~Jean Rostand

To forgive is human, to forget divine.

~James Grand

How often could things be remedied by a word. How often is it left unspoken.

~Norman Douglas

~

207

TASTES

Only those who aren't hungry are able to judge the quality of a meal.

~Alessandro Morandotti

Criticism is not just a question of taste, but of whose taste.

~James Grand

Even the greatest excellences tremble before the person of refined taste, and the most perfect lose their confidence.

~Baltasar Gracián

It is an insufferable fool who measures all things by his own opinion.

~Baltasar Gracián

Tastes are as abundant as faces and just as varied.

~Baltasar Gracián

~

Next to sound judgment, diamonds and pearls are the rarest things in the world.

~Jean de La Bruyère

Taste ripens at the expense of happiness.

~Jules Renard

When you have a taste for exceptional people you always end up meeting them everywhere.

~Pierre Mac Orlan

Taste is the only morality... Tell me what you like, and I'll tell you what you are.

~John Ruskin

TEMPTATION

Temptation laughs at the fool who takes it seriously.

> ~Chofetz Chaim

Show me a hero and I will write you a tragedy.

> ~F. Scott Fitzgerald

'Every man has his price.' This is not true. But for every man there exists a bait which he cannot resist swallowing. To win over certain people to something, it is only necessary to give it a gloss of love of humanity, nobility, gentleness, self~sacrifice – and there is nothing you cannot get them to swallow.

> ~Friedrich Nietzsche

The devil's boots don't creak.

> ~Scottish proverb

The heron's a saint when there are no fish about.

> ~Japanese Proverb

Better shun the bait than struggle in the snare.

> ~John Dryden

There are several good protections against temptations, but the surest is cowardice.

> ~Mark Twain

I can resist everything except temptation.

> ~Oscar Wilde

THANKFULNESS

A thankful heart is not only the greatest virtue, but the parent of all the other virtues.

~Cicero

~

Always remember to forget

The troubles that passed away,

But never forget to remember

The blessings that come each day.

~Anonymous

He is a wise man who does not grieve for the things which he has not, but rejoices for those which he has.

~Epictetus

It is more blessed to give than to receive; yet a noble nature can accept and be thankful.

~Johann August Strindberg

There is no debt so heavy to a grateful mind as a debt of kindness unpaid.

~Laurence Sterne

I have heard that God has two dwellings, one in heaven and the other in a meek and thankful heart.

~Izaak Walton

Almost everyone takes pleasure in repaying small obligations; many are thankful for moderate acts of kindness but scarcely anyone is thankful for great mercies.

~François Duc de la Rochefoucauld

'THE CRITICK'

Insects sting, not from malice,
but because they want to live.
It is the same with critics – they
desire our blood, not our pain.

~Friedrich Nietzsche

The only impeccable writers
are those that never wrote.

~William Hazlitt

It is much easier to recognize
error than to find truth; the
former lies on the surface, this
is quite manageable; the latter
resides in depth, and this quest
is not everyone's business.

~Johann Wolfgang von
Goethe

~

There are two things for which
animals are to be envied: they
know nothing of future evils, or
of what people say about them.

~ François-Marie
Arouet Voltaire

There is a small dose of revenge
in every complaint.

~Friedrich Nietzsche

Complainants are the greatest
persecutors.

~Samuel Butler

If you hear someone is speaking
ill of you, instead of trying to
defend yourself you should say:
'He obviously does not know
me very well, since there are so
many other faults he could have
mentioned'.

~Epictetus

Malice is a greater magnifying-
glass than kindness.

~Marquess of Halifax

211

The apple tree never asks the beech how he shall grow, nor the lion, the horse, how he shall take his prey.

~William Blake

Critics are like brushers of noblemen's clothes.

~George Herbert

There be some men are born only to suck out the poison of books.

~Ben Jonson

The man who does things makes mistakes, but he never makes the biggest mistake of all – doing nothing.

~Benjamin Franklin

'THE CROWD'

One can't live for everyone, more especially not for those with whom one wouldn't care to live.

~Johann Wolfgang von Goethe

Nothing is more disagreeable than a majority; for it consists of a few powerful people in the lead, rogues who are adaptable, weak people who assimilate with the rest, and the crowd that trundles along behind without the slightest notion of what it's after.

~Johann Wolfgang von Goethe

The crowd admires common foolishness and places no stock in excellent counsel.

~Baltasar Gracián

Careful observation has been pushed aside by an ill-conceived desire for imaginary applause.

~Baltasar Gracián

~

To be happy, we must not be too concerned with others.

~Albert Camus

213

THE EYES

One's eyes are what one is,
one's mouth what one
becomes.

> ~John Galsworthy

When indifferent, the eye takes
still photographs; when
interested, movies.

> ~Malcolm de Chazal

An intelligent person often
talks with his eyes.

> ~Anonymous

~

Beauty is how you feel inside,
and it reflects in your eyes. It is
not something physical.

> ~Sophia Loren

One's eyes are what one is;
one's mouth, what one
becomes.

> ~John Galsworthy

A man falls in love through his
eyes, a woman through her ears.

> ~W. Wyatt

THE FUTURE

Only man clogs his happiness
with care, destroying what is
with thoughts of what may be.

~John Dryden

Tomorrow is the day when
idlers work, and fools reform,
and mortal men lay hold on
heaven.

~Edward Young

The future is a mirror without
any glass in it.

~Xavier Forneret

I never think of the future; it
comes soon enough.

~Albert Einstein

I still lived in the future – a
habit which is the death of
happiness.

~Quentin Crisp

King Hassan, well beloved, was
wont to say

When aught went wrong, or
any project failed:

'Tomorrow, friends, will be
another day!'

And in that faith he slept and so
prevailed.

~James Buckham

~

You have brains in your head.
You have feet in your shoes.
You can steer yourself
Any direction you choose.

~Dr. Seuss

One should never place one's
trust in the future. It doesn't
deserve.

~André Chamson

215

Tomorrow is an old deceiver,
and his cheat never grows stale.

~Samuel Johnson

Tomorrow, do thy worst, for I
have lived today.

~Henry Fielding

The greater part of our lives is
spent in dreaming over the
morrow, and when it comes, it,
too, is consumed in the
anticipation of a brighter
morrow, and so the cheat is
prolonged, even to the grave.

~Mark Rutherford

The man least dependent upon
the morrow goes to meet the
morrow most cheerfully.

~Epicurus

Hardly anyone knows how
much is gained by ignoring the
future.

~Bernard de Fontenelle

When all else is lost, the future
still remains.

~Christian Bovee

Finish every day and be done
with it. You have done what
you could; some blunders and
absurdities crept in – forget
them as soon as you can.
Tomorrow is a new day. You
shall begin it well and serenely,
and with too high a spirit to be
encumbered with your old nonsense.

~Ralph Waldo Emerson

The strongest are those who
renounce their own times and
become a living part of those yet
to come. The strongest and the
rarest.

~ Milovan Đilas

The best thing about the future
is that is comes one day at a
time.

~Dean Acheson

The danger of the past was that men became slaves. The danger of the future is that men may become robots.

~Eric Fromm

There are two times in a man's life when he should not speculate – when he can't afford it, and when he can.

~Mark Twain

We often borrow from our tomorrows to pay our debts to our yesterdays.

~Kahlil Gibran

THE ILLUSION OF SAFETY

The lust for comfort murders the passion of the soul, and then walks grinning in the funeral.

~Kahlil Gibran

The desire for safety stands against every great and noble enterprise.

~Tacitus

~

If all that Americans want is security they can go to prison.

~Dwight Eisenhower

The most secure individual in our society is a prisoner serving a life sentence.

~Senator Joseph Ball

218

THE MORNING

A man must swallow a toad
every morning if he wishes to
be sure of finding nothing still
more disgusting before the day
is over.

> ~Sébastien-Roch Nicolas
> Chamfort

With every rising of the sun

Think of your life as just begun.

> ~Anonymous

One is wiser in the morning
than in the evening.

> ~Russian Proverb

Go to bed early, get up early –
this is wise.

> ~Mark Twain

THE PAST

There is no greater sorrow than to recall a happy time in the midst of wretchedness.

~Dante Alighieri

No past is dead for us, but only sleeping, love.

~Helen Hunt Jackson

Of all sad words of tongue or pen, the saddest are these: It might have been.

~John Greenleaf
Whittier

~

The illusion that times that were are better than those that are has probably pervaded all ages.

~Horace Greeley
(1811~1872)

Ne'er look for the birds of this year in the nests of the last.

~Miguel de Cervantes

Nor deem the irrevocable Past

As wholly wasted, wholly vain,

If, rising on its wrecks, at last

To something nobler we attain.

~Henry Wadsworth
Longfellow

Men are more like the times they live in than they are like their fathers.

~Ali Ibn-Abi-Talib

THE PRESENT

Enjoy yourself, drink, call the
life you live today your own –
but only that; the rest belongs
to chance.

~Euripides

Who controls the past controls
the future; who controls the
present controls the past.

~George Orwell

~Zach La Rocha

Whatever can happen at any
time can happen today.

~Seneca

Nothing should be treasured
more highly than the value of
the day.

~Johann Wolfgang von
Goethe

We are always getting ready to
live, but never living.

~Ralph Waldo Emerson

~

Nothing ever gets anywhere.
The earth keeps turning round
and gets nowhere. The moment
is the only thing that counts.

~Jean Cocteau

Nothing is worth more than this
day.

~Johann Wolfgang von
Goethe

The ideal never comes. Today
is the ideal for him who makes
it so.

~Horatio W. Dresser

That man is happiest who lives
from day to day and asks no
more, garnering the simple
goodness of life.

~Euripides

Make the most of today.
Translate your good intentions
into actual deeds.

~Grenville Kleiser

Seize the day, and put the least
possible trust in tomorrow.

~Horace

One today is worth two
tomorrows.

~Benjamin Franklin

Half of today is better than all of
tomorrow.

~Jean de La Fontaine

Yesterday is ashes; tomorrow
wood. Only today does the fire
burn brightly.

~Old Eskimo proverb

Everyman's life lies within the
present, for the past is spent and
down with, and the future is
uncertain.

~Marcus Aurelius

Look not mournfully into the
past, it comes not back again.
Wisely improve the present, it is
thine. Go forth to meet the
shadowy future without fear
and with a manly heart.

~Henry Wadsworth
Longfellow

Few of us ever live in the
present, we are forever
anticipating what is to come or
remembering what has gone.

~Louis L'Amour

Real generosity toward the
future lies in giving all to the
present.

~Albert Camus

Reflect upon your present
blessings, of which every man
has many – not on your past

misfortunes, of which all men have some.

~Charles Dickens

THINKING

It is unreasonable always to follow only reason.

> ~Karol Bunsch

~

Talking without thinking is like shooting without aiming.

> ~Zbigniew Herbert

Thoughts are the shadows of our feelings – always darker, emptier and simpler.

> ~Friedrich Nietzsche

We're only really thinking when we can't think out fully what we are thinking about!

> ~Johann Wolfgang von
> Goethe

Thought must be divided against itself before it can come to any knowledge of itself.

> ~Aldous Huxley

Great thoughts come from the heart.

> ~Marquis de
> Vauvenargues

The irrational is not necessarily unreasonable.

> ~Lewis Namier

Curiosity is one of the permanent and certain characteristics of a vigorous mind.

> ~Samuel Johnson

The voice of the intellect is a soft one, but it does not rest till it has gained a hearing.

> ~Sigmund Freud

There is a kinship, a kind of freemasonry, between all persons of intelligence, however antagonistic their moral outlook.

~Norman Douglas

A moment's insight is sometimes worth a life's experience.

~Oliver Wendell Holmes

When we are tired, we are attacked by ideas we conquered long ago.

~Friedrich Nietzsche

The mind cannot long act the role of the heart.

~François Duc de la Rochefoucauld

We think in generalities, but we live in detail.

~Alfred North Whitehead

Civilized man's brain is a museum of contradictory truths.

~Remy de Gourmont

Study without reflection is a waste of time; reflection without study is dangerous.

~Confucius

Liberty: one of imagination's most precious possessions.

~Ambrose Bierce

The unexamined life is not worth living.

~Plato

Among mortals second thoughts are the wisest.

~Euripides

To think is to live.

~Cicero

I think, therefore I am

(Cogito, ergo sum)

~Rene Descartes

The more unintelligent a man is,
the less mysterious existence
seems to him.

~Arthur Schopenhauer

You should pray for a sound
mind in a sound body.

~Juvenal

If you wish to advance into the
infinite, explore the finite in all
directions.

~Johann Wolfgang von
Goethe

One must look for one thing
only, to find many.

~Cesare Pavese

It is not certain that everything
is uncertain.

~Blaise Pascal

THIS MOMENT

**The greatest evil of our time –
which lets nothing come to
fruition – is, I think, that one
moment consumes the next,
wastes the day with that same
day and so is always living
from hand to mouth without
achieving anything of
substance.**

> ~Johann Wolfgang von
> Goethe

**No man is rich enough to buy
back his past.**

> ~Oscar Wilde

~

Seize the hour.

> ~Sophocles

Guard well your spare
moments. They are like uncut
diamonds. Discard them and
their value will never be known.

Improve them and they will
become the brightest gems in a
useful life.

> ~Ralph Waldo Emerson

The butterfly counts not months
but moments, and has time
enough.

> ~Rabindranath Tagore

In order to be utterly happy the
only thing necessary is to
refrain from comparing this
moment with other moments in
the past, which I often did not
fully enjoy because I was
comparing them with other
moments of the future.

> ~Andre Gide

But what minutes! Count them
by sensation, and not by
calendars, and each moment is a
day.

> ~Benjamin Disraeli

227

TIME

The early bird gets the worm, but the second mouse gets the cheese.

~Steven Wright

He who never hurries is always on time.

~Mikhail Bulgakov

There is always time to take more time.

~Augusto Roa Bastos

Punctuality is the virtue of the bored.

~Evelyn Waugh

Beware the barrenness of a busy life.

~Socrates

The really idle man gets nowhere; the perpetually busy does not get much further.

~H. Ogilvie

~

Punctuality is the thief of time.

~Oscar Wilde

Men talk of killing time, while time quietly kills them.

~Dion Boucicault

Ah! The clock is always slow; it is later than you think.

~Robert W. Service

Time is

Too slow for those wait,

Too swift for those who fear,

Too long for those who grieve,

228

Too short for those who rejoice.

But for those who love, time is not.

~Henry van Dyke

Time is one kind of robber whom the law does not strike at, and who steals what is most precious to men.

~Napoleon Bonaparte

Time is the subtle thief of youth.

~John Milton

Time is a sort of river passing events, and strong is its current; no sooner is a thing brought to sight than it is swept by and another takes its place, and this too will be swept away.

~Marcus Aurelius

The day is immeasurably long to him who knows not how to value and use it.

~Johann Wolfgang von Goethe

Time ripens all things: no man is born wise.

~Miguel de Cervantes

The life so short, the craft so long to learn.

~Geoffrey Chaucer

O gentlemen, the time of life is short!

~William Shakespeare

Procrastination is the thief of time.

~Edward Young

Time flies.

(Tempus fugit).

~Ovid

TRAVEL

A man travels the world over in search of what he needs and returns home to find it.

~George Moore

Everywhere is nowhere. When a person spends all this time in foreign travel, he ends by having many acquaintances, but no friends.

~Seneca

~

You're off to Great Places!
Today is your day!
Your mountain is waiting.
So . . . get on your way!

~Dr. Seuss

Arriving at each new city, the traveler finds again a past of his that he did not know he had: the foreignness of what you no longer are or no longer possess

lies in wait for you in foreign, unpossessed places.

~Italo Calvino

Though we travel the world over to find the beautiful, we must carry it with us or we find it not.

~Anonymous

Mid pleasures and palaces we may roam,

Be it ever so humble, there's no place like home.

~J.H. Payne

Worth seeing? Yes; but not worth going to see.

~Samuel Johnson

To travel hopefully is a better thing than to arrive.

~Robert Louis Stevenson

Always roaming with a hungry
heart.

~Robert Louis
Stevenson

I have traveled a good deal in
Concord.

~Henry David Thoreau

I travel not to go anywhere, but
to go.

~Robert Louis
Stevenson

May the road rise to meet you.
May the wind be always at your
back. May the sun shine warm
upon your face, the rains fall
soft upon your fields and, until
we meet again, may God hold
you in the palm of His hand.

~Irish Prayer

TRUTH

An error is the more dangerous
in proportion to the degree of
truth which it contains.

~Henri Frédéric Amiel

The most dangerous untruths
are truths slightly distorted.

~Georg Christoph
Lichtenberg

The truth is too simple: one
must always get there by a
complicated route.

~George Sand

Nothing is more damaging to a
new truth than an old error.

~Johann Wolfgang von
Goethe

Prudent people save one of
their ears for truth.

~Baltasar Gracián

The body never lies.

~Martha Graham

~

Truth for us nowadays is not
what is, but what others can be
brought to accept.

~Michel de Montaigne
(1533~1592)

Man is least himself when he
talks in his own person. Give
him a *mask* and he will tell the
truth.

~Oscar Wilde

Truth is such a rare thing, it is
delightful to tell it.

~Emily Dickinson

232

What probably distorts
everything in life is that one is
convinced that one is speaking
the truth because one says what
one thinks.

~Sacha Guitry

Truth is more of a stranger than
fiction.

~Mark Twain

Truth is too naked; she does not
inflame men.

~Jean Cocteau

Truth is the cry of all, but the
game of the few.

~Bishop Berkeley

If you shut your door to all
errors truth will be shut out.

~Rabindranath Tagore

You can find truth with logic if
you have already found truth
without it.

~G.K. Chesterton

What is now proved was once
only imagin'd.

~William Blake

To become properly acquainted
with a truth we must first have
disbelieved it, and disputed
against it.

~Baron Friedrich von
Hardenberg Novalis

Those who never retract their
opinions love themselves more
than they love the truth.

~Joseph Joubert

We are not satisfied to be right,
unless we can prove others to be
quite wrong.

~William Hazlitt

Truth is the safest lie.

~Yiddish proverb

Law is whatever is boldly
asserted and plausibly
maintained.

~Aaron Burr

All truths that are kept silent
become poison.

~Friedrich Nietzsche

A man had rather have a
hundred lies told of him than
one truth which he does not
wish should be told.

~Samuel Johnson

Truth above all, even when it
upsets and overwhelms us.

~Henri-Frederic Amiel

To work, to help, and to be
helped, to learn sympathy
through suffering, to learn faith
by perplexity, is to reach truth
through wonder.

~Phillips Brooks

Nothing is truer in a sense than
a funeral oration. It tells
precisely what the dead man
should have been.

~J. Vaperean

Love the truth but pardon the
error.

~Voltaire

A man should never be
ashamed to own that he has
been in the wrong, which is but
saying, in other words, that he
is wiser today than he was
yesterday.

~Jonathan Swift

~Alexander Pope

The certainties of one age are
the problems of the next.

~R.H. Tawney

VICE

Men are not punished for their sins, but by them.

> ~Frank McKinney
> Hubbard

All sins are attempts to fill voids.

> ~Simone Weil

Just as virtue is its own reward, vice is its own punishment.

> ~Baltasar Gracián

~

That which we call sin in others, is experiment for us.

> ~Ralph Waldo Emerson

No vice exists which does not pretend to be more or less like some virtue and which does not take advantage of this assumed resemblance.

> ~Jean de La Bruyère

There are some vices which only keep hold on us through other ones, and if we take the trunk away they come off like the branches.

> ~Blaise Pascal

Men imagine that they communicate their virtue or vice only by overt actions, and do not see that virtue or vice emit a breath every moment.

> ~Ralph Waldo Emerson

Melancholy, indeed, should be diverted by every means but drinking.

> ~Samuel Johnson

Of all the vices, drinking is the most incompatible with greatness.

~Sir Walter Scott

Men blush less for their crimes than for their weaknesses and vanity.

~Jean de La Bruyère

At the first cup man drinks wine, at the second wine drinks wine, at the third wine drinks man.

~Japanese Proverb

Bad men live that they may eat and drink, whereas good men eat and drink that they may live.

~Socrates

What were once vices are now the manners of the day.

~Seneca

We are often saved from exclusive addiction to a single vice by the possession of others.

~François Duc de la Rochefoucauld

A man does not mind being blamed for his faults, and being punished for them, and he patiently suffers much for them; but he becomes impatient if he is required to give them up.

~Johann Wolfgang von Goethe

Conscience warns us before it reproaches us.

~Comtesse Diane

We confess our faults in the plural, and deny them in the singular.

~Richard Fulke Greville

He that loses his conscience has nothing left worth keeping.

~Izaak Walton

~Robert Ingersoll

In nature there are neither
rewards nor punishments; there
are consequences.

VIRTUE

Three things make a marvel, and are at the acme of true nobility: fertile intelligence, deep powers of judgment, and a pleasant, relevant taste.

~Baltasar Gracián

Virtue is a chain of all perfections, the center of all happiness. She makes you prudent, discreet, shrewd, sensible, wise, brave, cautious, honest, happy, praiseworthy, true... a universal hero.

~Baltasar Gracián

Virtue is the sun of the lesser world, and its hemisphere is a good conscience. It is so lovely that it wins God's grace and that of others.

~Baltasar Gracián

There is nothing as lovable as virtue, nor as hateful as vice.

~Baltasar Gracián

Virtue alone is for real; all else is sham.

~Baltasar Gracián

Talent and greatness depend on virtue, not fortune.

~Baltasar Gracián

Only virtue is sufficient unto herself.

~Baltasar Gracián

What a sad age this is, when virtue is rare and malice is common.

~Baltasar Gracián

There are no perfectly honorable men; but every true man has one main point of honor and a few minor ones.

~George Bernard Shaw

Three things make one blessed: saintliness, wisdom, and prudence.

~Baltasar Gracián

~

Virtue is a stranger in this world; and boundless egoism, cunning, and malice are always the order of the day. It is wrong to deceive the young on this point, for it will only make them feel later on that their teachers were the first to deceive them.

~Arthur Schopenhauer

Virtues and vices are of a strange nature; for the more we have, the fewer we think we have.

~Anonymous

Perhaps, for worldly success, we need virtues that make us loved and faults that make us feared.

~Joseph Joubert

Vice and sins are a deadly poison; but virtues and good works are a healing medicine.

~St. Francis of Assisi

Vice is its own reward.

~John Dryden

Virtue is a kind of health, beauty and good habit of the soul.

~Plato

Some rise by sin, and some by virtue fall.

~William Shakespeare

Our virtues are most frequently but the vices in disguise.

~François Duc de la Rochefoucauld

WAR & PEACE

A fine retreat is as good as a gallant attack.

~Baltasar Gracián

Patriotism is the last refuge of a scoundrel.

~Samuel Johnson

In war, there are no unwounded soldiers.

~José Narosky

War does not determine who is right – only who is left.

~Bertrand Russell

At the bottom of a good deal of bravery … lurks a miserable cowardice. Men will face powder and steel because they cannot face public opinion.

~Edwin H. Chapin

Few wage war fairly.

~Baltasar Gracián

Peace, commerce, and honest friendship for all nations, entangling alliances with none.

~Thomas Jefferson (1778)

There never was a good war or a bad peace.

~Benjamin Franklin

War is sweet to those who have not experienced it.

~Erasmus

War is only a cowardly escape from the problems of peace.

~Thomas Mann

Lord, make me an instrument of your peace:

Where there is hatred, let me sow love,

Where there is injustice, pardon,

Where there is doubt, faith,

Where there is despair, hope,

Where there is dark, light,

Where there is sadness, joy.

~St. Francis of Assisi

~

Malicious men may die, but malice never.

~Jean-Baptiste Poquelin de Molière

There is a passion for hunting something deeply implanted in the human breast.

~Charles Dickens

Those who know the least obey the best.

~George Farquhar

Even in a declaration of war one observes the rules of politeness.

~Prince Otto von Bismarck

If the rich could hire other people to die for them, the poor could make a wonderful living.

~Yiddish proverb

It is the province of the historian to find out, not what was, but what it is. Where a battle has been fought, you will find nothing but the bones of men and beasts; where a battle is being fought, there are hearts beating.

~Henry David Thoreau

Speak softly and carry a big stick.

~Theodore Roosevelt

I shall say it again and again.
Your boys are not going to be
sent into any foreign wars.

~Franklin Delano
Roosevelt (1940)

I am sick and tired of war. Its
glory is all moonshine. It is
only those who have never fired
a shot nor heard the shrieks and
groans of the wounded who cry
aloud for blood, more
vengeance, more desolation.
War is hell.

~William Tecumseh
Sherman

There are no atheists in the fox
holes.

~William Thomas
Cummings

A hell of a way to make a living.

~Anonymous

If Christian nations were
nations of Christians, there
would be no wars.

~Soame Jenyns

War would end if the dead
could return.

~Stanley Baldwin

The first panacea for a
mismanaged nation is inflation
of the currency. The second is
war. Both bring a temporary
prosperity; both bring a
permanent ruin.

~Ernest Hemingway

Peace cannot be kept by force.
It can only be achieved by
understanding.

~Albert Einstein

Non-violence is not meant
merely for the rishis and saints.
It is meant for the common
people as well. Non-violence is
the law of the brute.

~Mahatma Gandhi

I am a man of peace. I believe in peace. But I do not want peace at any price. I do not want the peace that you find in stone; I do not want the peace that you find in the grave: but I do want the peace which you find embedded in the human breast, which is exposed to the arrows of the whole world, but which is protected from all harm by the power of Almighty God.

~Mahatma Gandhi

Peace is a daily, a weekly, a monthly process, gradually changing opinions, slowly eroding old barriers, quietly building new structures. And however undramatic the pursuit of peace, the pursuit must go on.

~John F. Kennedy

There can never be peace between nations until there is the true peace which is within the souls of men.

~ Elisabeth Kübler-Ross

Is it progress if a cannibal uses knife and fork?

~ Stanislaus J. Lec

WISDOM & FOLLY

Voices become louder when
understanding diminishes.

~Friedrich Georg Jünger

None so empty as those that
are full of themselves.

~Benjamin Whichcote

Mingle some brief folly with
your wisdom.

~Horace

No matter how far you have
gone on a wrong road, turn
back.

~Turkish proverb

From the errors of others, a
wise man corrects his own.

~Publilius Syrus

Don't use the conduct of a fool
as a precedent.

~Talmud

Wise men learn by other men's
mistakes, fools by their own.

~H.G. Bohn

A wise man's question
contains half the answer.

~Solomon Ibn Gabirol

It is the property of fools, to be
always judging.

~Thomas Fuller

~

The art of being wise is the art
of knowing what to overlook.

~William James

244

He must be a thorough fool,
who can learn nothing from his
own folly.

~Julius Hare

The first step towards madness
is to think oneself wise.

~Fernando de Rojas

All this worldly wisdom was
once the unamiable heresy of
some wise man.

~Henry Thoreau

They condemn what they do
not understand.

~Cicero

A man who is his own doctor
has a fool for his patient.

~Anonymous

A fellow who is always
declaring he's no fool, usually
has his suspicions.

~Anonymous

For fools rush in where angels
fear to tread.

~Alexander Pope

A fool must now and then be
right, by chance.

~William Cowper

Wisdom never lies.

~Homer

WOMEN

Woman inspires us to great things, and prevents us from achieving them.

~Alexandre Dumas

~

There are beautiful flowers that are scentless, and beautiful women that are unlovable.

~Houellé

Once a woman has given her heart you can never get rid of the rest of her.

~Sir John Vanbrugh

The great question that has never been answered, and which I have not yet been able to answer despite my thirty years of research into the feminine soul is: What does a woman want?

~Sigmund Freud

Next to the wound, what women make best is the bandage.

~Barbey D'Aurevilly

A beautiful woman should break her mirror early.

~ Baltasar Gracián

The man's desire is for the woman; but the woman's desire is rarely other than for the desire of the man.

~Samuel Taylor Coleridge

Woman's vanity demands that a man be more than a happy husband.

~Friedrich Nietzsche

How many girls are there for whom great beauty has been of no use but to make them hope for a great fortune?

~Jean de La Bruyère

A mother takes twenty years to make a man of her boy, and another woman makes a fool of him in twenty minutes.

~Robert Frost

When women kiss, it always reminds me of prize fighters shaking hands.

~H.L. Mencken

There are two ways to handle a woman, and nobody knows either of them.

~Kim Hubbard

The two divinest things in this world has got,

A lovely woman in a rural spot.

~Leigh Hunt

...Can't live with them, or without them.

~Aristophanes

247

WORDS

The finest thought runs the risk of being irretrievably forgotten if it is not written down.

> ~Arthur Schopenhauer

Silken words, delivered gently. Arrows go through the body: bad words, through the soul.

> ~Baltasar Gracián

Words are loaded pistols.

> ~Jean Paul Sartre

~

Some sentences release their poisons only after years.

> ~Elias Canetti

One always speaks badly when one has nothing to say.

> ~Francois Marie Arouet de Voltaire

The great consolation in life is to say what one thinks.

> ~Francois Marie Arouet de Voltaire

All truths that are kept silent become poisonous.

> ~Friedrich Nietzsche

There is much to be said in favour of modern journalism. By giving us the opinions of the uneducated, it keeps us in touch with the ignorance of the community.

> ~Oscar Wilde

Advertising has annihilated the power of the most powerful adjectives.

> ~Paul Valéry

When gossip grows old it becomes myth.

>~Stanislaus J. Lec

It is the proof of high culture to say the greatest matters in the simplest way.

>~Ralph Waldo Emerson

True eloquence consists of saying all that should be said, and that only.

>~François Duc de la Rochefoucauld

I have made this letter longer than usual because I lack the time to make it short.

>~Blaise Pascal

A blow with a word strikes deeper than a blow with a sword.

>~Robert Burton

WORK

Shun those studies in which the work that results dies with the worker.

~Leonardo da Vinci

The great use of life is to spend it for something that will outlast it.

~William James

Oh Lord, thou givest us everything, at the price of an effort.

~Leonardo da Vinci

To the man who himself strives earnestly, God also lends a helping hand.

~Aeschylus

Work is often the father of pleasure.

~Voltaire

The goal of war is peace; of business, leisure.

~Aristotle

Work keeps us from three great evils: boredom, vice and need.

~Voltaire

To do two things at once is do neither.

~Publilius Syrus

~

Few men make themselves masters of the things they write or speak.

~John Selden

Cut off from the worship of the divine, leisure becomes laziness and work inhuman.

~John Piper

One chops the wood, the other does the grunting.

~Yiddish proverb

Quality is not an act. It is a habit.

~Aristotle

A well-spent day brings happy sleep.

~Leonardo da Vinci

To do great work, a man must be very idle as well as very industrious.

~Samuel Butler

If you cannot work with love but only with distaste it is better that you should leave your work and sit at the gates of the temple and take alms of those who work with joy.

~Kahlil Gibran

Nothing is ever accomplished by a committee unless it consists of three members, one of whom happens to be sick and the other absent.

~Hendrik Willem Van Loon

A committee is a thing which takes a week to do what one good man can do in an hour.

~Elbert Hubbard

Committee: a group of men who keep minutes and waste hours.

~Anonymous

When love and skill work together, expect a masterpiece.

~John Ruskin

It is better to deserve without receiving than to receive without deserving.

~Robert Ingersoll

To be idle and to be poor have always been reproaches and therefore every man endeavors with his utmost care to hide his poverty from others and his idleness from himself.

~Samuel Johnson

When you see what some girls marry, you realize how they must hate to work for a living.

~H. Rouchard

Our chief want in life is somebody who shall makes us do what we can.

~Ralph Waldo Emerson

Nothing is worth doing unless the consequences may be serious.

~George Bernard Shaw

The test of a vocation is the love of the drudgery it involves.

~Anonymous

The most desirable thing in life after health and modest means is leisure with dignity.

~Cicero

Leisure is the mother of Philosophy.

~Thomas Hobbes

A broad margin of leisure is as beautiful in a man's life as in a book.

~Henry David Thoreau

Nothing can exceed the vanity of our existence but folly of our pursuits.

~Oliver Goldsmith

All work, even cotton spinning, is noble; work is alone noble.

~Thomas Carlyle

For men must work, and women must weep,

And there's little to earn and many to keep.

~Charles Kingsley

WORRY

Worry never robs tomorrow of its sorrow, but only saps today of its strength.

~A.J. Cronin

A day of worry is more exhausting than a day of work.

~John Lubbock

Worry is a complete cycle of inefficient thought revolving around a pivotal fear.

~Anonymous

Worry is a state of mind based on fear.

~Napoleon Hill

Happy the man who has broken the chains which hurt the mind, and has given up worrying, once and for all.

~Ovid

As a rule, what is out of sight disturbs men's minds more seriously than what they see.

~Julius Caesar

Cast all your care on God! That anchor holds.

~Lord Alfred Tennyson

You'll break the worry habit the day you decide **you can meet and master the worse that can happen to you.**

~Arnold Glasow

~

It is not life and wealth and power that enslave men, but the cleaving to life and wealth and power.

~Buddha

254

Every moment of worry
weakens the soul for its daily
combat.

~Henry Wood

It is for the superfluous we
sweat.

~Socrates

Consider, Sir, how insignificant
this will appear a twelve-month
hence.

~Samuel Johnson

It is pleasant to recall past
troubles.

~Cicero

YOUTH

Nothing has a stronger influence psychologically on their environment, and especially on their children, than the unlived life of the parents.

~Carl Gustav Jung

~

We find delight in the beauty and happiness of children that makes the heart too big for the body.

~Ralph Waldo Emerson

It is better to waste one's youth than to do nothing with it at all.

~Georges Courteline

Allow children to be happy in their own way, for what better way will they ever find?

~Samuel Johnson

The fundamental defect of fathers is that they want their children to be a credit to them.

~Bertrand Russell

There are no illegitimate children, only illegitimate parents.

~Leon Yankwich

If a child lives with approval, he learns to like himself.

~Dorothy Law Nolte

To establish oneself in the world, one does all one can to seem established there already.

~ François Duc de la Rochefoucauld

256

MY CONDENSED WISDOM

BY

KALE MICHAEL PREWITT

Moderation in all things,
except moderation.

~

The only ones that love the
selfish are themselves, and
even that appears false.

~

The immediacy incrementally
drowns out the ideal.

~

A gentle spirit, a kind face and
a quick smile are the only
passports you need to travel
anywhere in the world.

~

We should wish for thicker
skin and softer hearts.

~

Paradoxically, our
confrontations make us closer
in the end.

~

Don't let those who pursue
goodness and truth in the
wrong name, dissuade you
from striving for what is
virtuous.

~

Perhaps the best nationalists
are the travelers and
expatriates.

~

I always love my country the
most when I'm furthest from it.

~

How many things seemed like
a good idea in the particular,
only to be disproved on a mass
scale?

~

Is all truth in life a paradox?

~

Closeness causes cuts and
calluses, yet also kinship and
community.

~

Can a changed man never
regress?

~

Ironically, shallowness always
lies readily apparent.

~

Man can find boredom in
every environment, and also
fascination.

~

A wise creature once told me,
'Adapt!' And I'm thankful I
listened.

~

Perhaps we should perfect our
understanding to comprehend
that there is no such thing as
perfection.

~

Perfect humility is facing the
world with pride despite being
completely humbled.

~

Sometimes life has a way of
forcing us to become content
with less. But the real test lies
in whether or not we can be

content with less when more becomes available.

~

Don't judge others to be judgers.

~

The beauty of art is that it can tell us not only the artist's story… but ours as well. Left to our own interpretation, we also are involved in the creation. To divulge all the piece's secrets, the artist robs us of our own discoveries. No matter how perfect a work, it is always half finished and left to the interpreter to finish.

~

You either make decisions or you don't,
And life moves on with or without you.
The choice of indecision
Is perhaps the most impactful of all decisions.

~

Happiness is contentment; most are not content to learn this.

ACKNOWLEDGEMENTS

Auden, W. H., & Kronenberger, L. (1981). *The Viking book of aphorisms : a personal selection.* Harmondsworth, Middlesex, England: Penguin Books.

Bachelder, L. (1968). *Time for reflection.* Mount Vernon, NY: Peter Pauper Press.

Cook, J. (1999). *The book of positive quotations.* New York: Gramercy Books.

Deger, S., & Gibson, L. A. (2009). *The little book of positive quotations.* Minneapolis, MN: Fairview Press.

Douglas, A., & Strumpf, M. (1989). *Webster's new world best book of aphorisms.* New York: Webster's NewWorld : Distributed by Prentice Hall.

Geary, J. (2007). *Geary's guide to the world's great aphorists.* New York: Bloomsbury : Distributed by Holtzbrinck Publishers.

Geary, J. (2005). *The world in a phrase : a brief history of the aphorism.* New York: Bloomsbury : Distributed to the trade by Holtzbrinck.

Goethe, J. W. (1998). *Maxims and reflections.* London: Penguin Books.

Gracián y Morales, B. (1991). *The art of worldly wisdom : a pocket oracle; translated by Christopher Maurer.* New York: Doubleday.

Gross, J. (1987). *The Oxford book of aphorisms.* Oxford: Oxford University Press.

Peterson, G. (1968). *Proverbs to live by; truths that live in words.* Kansas City, MO: Hallmark Editions.

Pinkey, M. (2002). *Pocket positives for our times.* Five Mile Press.

Woods, H. F. (1950). *American sayings; famous phrases, slogans and aphroisms.* New York: Perma Giants.

INDEX OF AUTHORS